IMAGES OF ENGL

AROUND
LEIGH

EQUO PEDE PROPERA

IMAGES OF ENGLAND

AROUND
LEIGH

TONY ASHCROFT AND NICHOLAS WEBB
FROM THE COLLECTIONS OF
WIGAN HERITAGE SERVICE

TEMPUS

Frontispiece: Arms granted to Leigh Municipal Borough, 1899. The quarterings consist of a spearhead (Westleigh), a mullet (Pennington), a shuttle (Bedford), and a sparrowhawk (Atherton). The first three townships were combined with part of Atherton to form an urban district in 1894 and subsequently the new borough. The crest is a bear's paw grasping a spearhead, representing respectively the Powys family (Lord Lilford), and the Urmstons of Westleigh. The motto 'Aequo Pede Propera', means 'To Make Progress Steadily'.

First published 1996
This edition published 2003

Tempus Publishing Limited
The Mill, Brimscombe Port,
Stroud, Gloucestershire, GL5 2QG

British Library Cataloguing in Publication Data.
A catalogue record for this book is available from the British Library.

ISBN 0 7524 3021 1

Typesetting and origination by Tempus Publishing Limited
Printed in Great Britain by Midway Colour Print, Wiltshire

Contents

In 1914 The National Relief Fund (also known as the Prince of Wales Fund) was established to help needy families. Here a group of local children prepares to collect money.

Beer barrels, pulled by dray horses, returning to George Shaw's brewery, Brewery Lane. This scene, captured around 1900, also shows a rag and bone cart.

Introduction

Leigh is one of Lancashire's historic small towns. As the centre of an ancient ecclesiastical parish its church embraced the neighbouring towns of Atherton and Tyldesley. Leigh was the scene of a skirmish in the Civil War, the district siding with parliament against the king. Its rich dairy country produced a local delicacy – the Leigh cheese – and before the Industrial Revolution the people practised traditional trades such as hand-loom weaving and nail-making. Linens and fustians made in Leigh were important before the large cotton mills came to employ so many thousands of men and women in Victorian times. Silk-weaving, too, was developed in the nineteenth century and had only just died out when our grandparents were young.

The coming of the canals helped the infant coal industry grow to be one of Leigh's major employers by the early 1900s, and although mining has now disappeared virtually without trace its memory lingers on. Engineering, notably iron founding, was the other of Leigh's big three industries, and this has survived into the modern age.

Several illustrated histories of Leigh have been published over the years. Most of these, however, are out of print and in any case only cover one or other aspects of the town's life. The purpose of this book is to present a comprehensive selection of photographs and other illustrations capturing the spirit of the place. There are sections devoted to people at work and at play, and others devoted to the public and ceremonial life of Leigh. Transport, education and domestic life are also covered. The book concludes with a selection of artistic studies of town and country scenes made by Dr Wynne, and a look at some of Leigh's personalities.

All the illustrations are drawn from Wigan Heritage Service's own collections. These have been patiently built up over the years by the efforts of staff and public alike, and most of the items used in this book have been donated or deposited by people anxious to ensure that part of their local heritage should be preserved. It is hoped that this publication will stimulate the further deposit of material.

The compilers have taken particular care to find illustrations that have not appeared in print before, and it is believed that this applies to the bulk of the book. Readers are thus presented with a genuinely fresh look at Leigh's past.

The geographical area covered by the book consists primarily of the former Municipal Borough. Whilst the ecclesiastical parish of Leigh included Astley, Atherton, Tyldesley and Leigh itself, for local government purposes all these were separate townships. Leigh town was divided between Bedford, Pennington and Westleigh townships, and these were brought together in 1875 to form the Leigh Local Board. In 1894 this became the Urban District and finally the council petitioned successfully for borough status which was granted in 1899 – the coat of arms is illustrated here. Part of Atherton, including The Avenue, originally extended to Leigh town centre, but this was annexed to Leigh in 1894. Thus the borough area prior to 1974 covered the ancient townships of Bedford (which up to the mid-Victorian period was almost a separate settlement), Pennington and Westleigh, together with a small part of Atherton.

One or two illustrations have also been included from the Lowton and Hindley Green areas, which traditionally have looked to Leigh as a market and trade centre. Indeed, Lowton was included in the former Leigh Rural District which existed between 1894 and 1933.

one

Civic
Pride

Above: The foundation stone of Leigh's new Town Hall was laid on 24 October 1904 by the Mayor, Alderman Henry Cowburn JP.

Left: John Fairclough JP, was born at Stone House on 19 July 1854. He became a partner in the firm of Fairclough Brothers, builders merchants, established by his grandfather John. He was associated with both Leigh Local Board and Urban District Council and in 1899 was elected as first Mayor of the new Borough. He was a representative of the trustees of France's Charity, a manager of the Savings Bank and an Associate of the Royal College of Organists. For many years he was organist at St Joseph's Church and also first President of Leigh Catholic Club. On 16 September 1919 John Fairclough became the second honorary freeman of the Borough. He died at his home, 155 Church Street, Leigh, on 4 July 1923.

Right: Mayor's Chain. The Mayoral regalia were given soon after the incorporation of the Borough. People were disappointed when the first Mayor John Fairclough attended church on Mayor's Sunday dressed as an ordinary gentleman. Shortly thereafter, on 17 August 1900, a gold badge (orna-mented with the Borough Arms), the mace and sword, mayor's monogram and miniature pictures of Leigh Parish Church, Market Place and Technical School, were presented to the Mayor by his Deputy Alderman T. R. Greenough. The second Mayor was Alderman George Shaw, the brewer. He appeared in full robe and cocked hat, which were given subsequently to his successors. His family presented the Mayor and his successors with this gold chain, to which the badge was attached.

Below: The scene in Market Street on 24 July 1907 when crowds gathered to see the official opening of Leigh's new Town Hall. Notice the gaily decorated tram car in the background.

The Council Chamber in Leigh Town Hall, showing the stained glass windows that were presented to the town by R. T. Marsh Esq. JP and unveiled on 25 June 1908 by the Mayor (Cllr G. Hunter JP). The lower lights depict local industries: weaving, spinning, commerce, education, engineering and mining. The upper lights contain the arms of the following local families. From left to right: Shuttleworth, Atherton, Bradshaw, Tyldesley, Mort and Urmston.

A procession of Leigh councillors on a Mayoral Sunday in the early 1900s. They were probably parading in Railway Road on the way to the parish church.

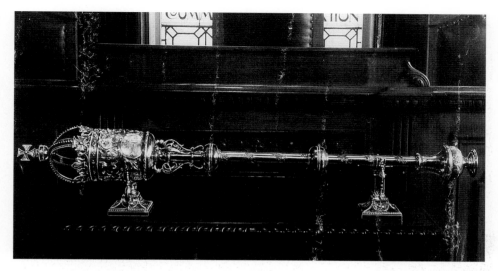

The mace which is 56 inches in length is of silver gilt. The mace head is divided by shields bearing the arms of Leigh, the monogram of the donor and the letter 'L' for Leigh. Four figures represent spinning, weaving, mining and iron founding. The shaft is divided by knops. The foot knop bears the inscription: – 'Presented to the Corporation of Leigh on the occasion of the opening of the new Town Hall, 24 July 1907, by Councillor W. Horrocks JP, Mayor 1902-3, 1906-7.

To commemorate George V's Silver Jubilee, Leigh Town Council decided in 1935 to erect four bungalows for aged people (to be let at a nominal rent of 3s), at the corner of Platt Fold Road and Holden Road. The first tenants were: Mr and Mrs Boydell, Mr and Mrs W. Dickinson, Mr and Mrs J. Phillips, Mr and Mrs E. Hardman. The photograph shows the Mayor (Cllr W. Blackshaw JP, CC) accompanied by the Mayoress officially opening the Jubilee Bungalows in March 1936. Mr Granville Shaw represented the builders, who presented the mayor with a gold key.

The Maternity Home at Stone House, St Helens Road, Leigh, was officially opened on 2 March 1927. Once the residence of Dr James Hayes, it had been given to the Corporation for a nominal sum. Since then it had been used as a Child Welfare Clinic. Another wing was added for midwifery purposes. Cllr T. R. Greenough JP (Chairman of the Health Committee) is seen presenting the Mayoress (Mrs W. Hilton) with a silver vase to commemorate the opening. Miss Roberts (Matron) is shown next to the Mayor (Cllr W. Hilton).

On 2 July 1921 Firs Park was officially opened by the Earl of Derby. Sir John H. Holden presented a gold key to the Earl as memento of the day's proceedings. As a director of Tunnicliffe & Hampsons, cotton spinners, who had given the site, Sir John handed over the park to the Corporation.

LEIGH, TYLDESLEY AND ATHERTON PREPARED

A.R.P. ARRANGEMENTS AT LEIGH

MAYOR'S IMPORTANT STATEMENT

There was no discussion of civic affairs at the monthly meeting of Leigh Town Council on Tuesday, the whole of the time being taken up by the Mayor (Counc. T. R. Greenough, J.P.), who read a long statement on A.R.P. preparations.

Counc. Battersby invited the Mayor to make a statement for public information as to what preparation has been made, what is being done, and what steps are yet to be taken to ensure as far as humanly possible the safety of every inhabitant in the borough in certain eventualities. He asked what were the changes made in the normal routine of various departments in order to cope with the work (e.g., clinics for first-aid posts), and if there were any deficiencies remaining in A.R.P. services (staff), and if so, what were the requirements in personnel.

The Mayor said the County Council was the scheme-making authority for air raid precautions for the borough and the Town Council had to render every assistance to the County authority and carry out schemes approved by them. The Council was the authority responsible for the auxiliary fire services. For many months past the various departments of the Corporation had been very active making arrangements so that in an emergency the safety of the public and the buildings in the town would, so far as was humanly possible, be safeguarded. With this end in view in September, 1938, an air raid precautions scheme was prepared which provides for the following services: Warning signals, control headquarters and report centre, first-aid posts, first-aid parties, ambulance services, rescue and demolition parties, decontamination squads, road repair squads, the provision of public shelters. In addition the County police had organized an extensive air raid wardens service. The warning signals were situate at Parsonage colliery, Bickershaw colliery, Anchor Cable works, Wood End colliery, Butts Corn Mill and Railway Inn, St. Helens-rd., and no matter what the prevailing wind might be the signals could be heard in every direction. In addition to the sirens the air raid wardens would patrol the town blowing whistles as a sign that an air raid might take place.

If these signals were given, the public were earnestly asked, for their own safety and the safety of the town generally to carry out the directions which had been given in the national Press and in the public information leaflets.

The operation of the scheme was based on a central control established in the basement at the Town Hall where the officers responsible for the various services would be represented. This department, known as the report centre, would receive, through the medium of the air raid wardens' service and the police, reports of any injuries to property or persons and would at once be able to send the assistance required.

The Mayor went on to give further details printed in another column, and said provision of shelters for the protection of the public had been made in various parts of the town to accommodate approximately 1,490 persons.

Volunteers were still required in order to bring the establishment up to strength and to create the necessary reserve.

The Auxiliary Fire Service was mobilized on Friday evening. The retained staff were called in for permanent duty and enough A.F.S. to man the three sub-stations. This entailed engaging 36 firemen and six officers on full time. Six permanent watch room attendants had been engaged (four ex-Service men and two women) for the chief station. The professional staff had not yet been augmented and the fire superintendent stated that a further five permanent watch room attendants were necessary. The total number of A.F.S. recruited at the present time was 201. It was possible for every street to be reviewed every seven minutes. Auxiliary Fire Stations had been established at Parsonage Farm, Westleigh Butts Corn Mill and at the Firs Maternity Home. A Watching Post was established at Pennington. Seventeen auxiliary fire pumps (six being of the heavy type) and a considerable quantity of hose and other equipment had been received. All the services were now and had been for some days standing by at their posts 24 hours to the day ready for action.

The normal routine of the various departments had materially suffered and most of the members of the staffs had been almost fully occupied with A.R.P. work during the last ten days. All departments affected had had to concentrate on perfecting as far as possible the A.R.P. services for which they were responsible and consequently their ordinary services had received little or no attention.

The Clinics had to be temporarily suspended—Stone House is being used as a first-aid post and the usual distribution of food is being carried out by the health department at the Town Hall—the other clinics were also being used for the distribution of food. The School Medical Services were automatically in abeyance, as the schools were closed

War a Futile Thing

Counc. Battersby expressed thanks to the Mayor for his exhaustive statement and said the staff had been working full time. All employees able to do something had given their services. None of them expected at the last Council meeting that they would be plunged into war, which would bring ruin, misery and carnage and he did not think there was a member of the Council who was not opposed to war, which was a futile way of settling disputes. The rule of force never won, although it might seem for a time to be triumphant. They had to look at home and see that everything was done for the welfare of the people that it was possible to do. It did not mean that they were afraid, perturbed, or perplexed, but they wanted to be sure that all that could be done was being done to save life. They would go on with that steadfast courage and calm determinedness to do their duty in the midst of these difficult days. He was sure every member would do all he could to promote England's cause and help it forward.

Counc. Bratt raised an interesting point when he asked were the shelters available day and night. He asked for a statement as to when the public were allowed to use them.

Ald. Higenbottam said the shelters in basements of public-houses were intended for day-time raids only.

Counc. Bratt said they did not want people rushing about the streets in their night attire if the shelters were closed.

Counc. Hourigan also pointed out that shops in Bradshawgate used as shelters closed at 7-30 p.m. If that meant the shelters were closed also then the posters outside were misleading.

The Mayor said the matter would be looked into immediately. The times would be marked on the posters outside the shelters when they could be used.

Counc. Parr said he wished to remind his colleagues that the country had only been at war for 56 hours and they could not reasonably expect 100 per cent safety in that time. He did not think the people were expecting that. They must complete what had been going on.

THE MAYOR, COUNC. T. R. GREENOUGH

If they were deficient it was certainly not the fault of the officials of the Council. All that was humanly possible had been done, and it was a great credit to all who had had charge of those matters.

Confound the Critics

Counc. Morgan added his tribute, and said the statement would certainly confound the critics, many of whom were about.

Counc. Bamford also said that credit was due to the officials of the Corporation, who were doing all they could to provide shelter and service for as many as possible. That was the first duty of the Corporation, but he felt that a similar duty was placed on every person in Leigh—to do all they could for themselves. They as a Council could only go so far. It was physically and financially an impossibility to provide shelter for 45,000 people. Each man and woman in Leigh had a responsibility, and that responsibility should be accepted and not all of it left to the Council.

Counc. Haseldine suggested that each householder should draw enough water—especially seeing that there was no shortage—to last a day or two, so that if anything happened to the reservoirs they would be sure of a supply.

Tributes to Staff

Referring to the Watch and Cemetery Committee's reports on the parks and cemetery, Ald. W. Collier said they were very pleased with the condition they found both in. The parks were up to the standard—if not better—than ever before. Great credit was reflected on Mr. Dyer and his staff. He hoped the public of Leigh would continue to use the parks during these distressing times. They could try to forget what they were going through by paying a visit to the parks. The cemetery, Ald. Collier added, looked better than it had done for a number of years. Credit was due to Mr. Bishop and his staff, who had made a considerable improvement at the entrance.

Housing Scheme

A sub-committee of the housing committee reported that they had considered the question of carrying out plastering work by direct labour in connexion with future housing schemes, and having regard to the capital expenditure which would have to be incurred in the purchase of necessary plant and to the fact that the building programme is nearing completion, they recommended that no alteration be made in the present system. It was resolved that the recommendations be approved and adopted, and that the Town Clerk inform the Leigh branch of the National Association of Operative Plasterers of the decision.

The committee approved and adopted estimates for the cost of the erection of 250 houses on the Thompson-st. (No. 2) site. The Town Clerk was authorized to make application to the Minister of Health for consent to the borrowing by the Council of the sum of £13,312, the estimated cost of street works, sewers, and fencing on the site. Sanction is also being sought for the erection of the houses by direct labour, and to the borrowing of the sum of £108,936.

The transport committee have decided on several important changes in their department. Tenders are to be invited for the supply of five double-deck buses of the totally enclosed type. One of the three buses to be taken out of service is to be retained and adapted as a break-down lorry. The washing plant at the garage is to be modernized at an estimated cost of £50. Two passenger shelters are to be overhauled and repainted.

At the meeting of the Committee the transport manager reported on a census of passengers taken on the Warrington-rd. bus route particularly as it affected the service to and from Dakins Lea.

After making an inspection of the parks and cemetery, the respective committees have expressed their appreciation of the manner in which they have been kept by the superintendent and registrar and their staffs.

At a special meeting of the Town Council on Tuesday evening the proceedings of a meeting of the General Purposes Committee on Saturday were confirmed.

The Town Clerk and the chief officials of the various departments verbally reported as to the steps taken by them with regard to air raid precautions. It was resolved that the Borough Surveyor prepare and seek the immediate approval of the County Council to a scheme for the provision of public air raid shelters in the borough.

During the continuance of the present state of emergency the Chairman of each committee of the Corporation's services dealing with air raid precautions (except public utility supplies) will meet each morning to review the position and a report will be made to the General Purposes Committee from time to time. The Building Manager was authorized to adapt the basement of the town hall under the health department as an air raid shelter to provide accommodation for the Council's staff at the town hall and the tenants of the shops thereunder.

The Town Clerk reported that he had received instructions from the Food (Defence Plans) Department of the Board of Trade to the effect that it was now necessary to set up a Food Control Committee for the borough, and submitted nominations received by him from the various associations of food trades. It was resolved that the following persons be appointed a Food Control Committee for the borough for a period of one year:—Mr. John Gregory, sen., retail grocer; Mr. Ralph Hindley, retail butcher; Mr. R. Howarth, general manager Leigh Co-operative Society; Counc. W. Kearney and Mr. F. Palmer, representing other retail food trades; the Mayor, the Deputy-Mayor, Ald. Higenbottam, Councillors Blackshaw, Bratt, Gough, Horrocks, Morgan, Mrs. Greenough (the Mayoress), and Mrs. Newton (the Deputy-Mayoress).

The Town Clerk reported that it was proposed to introduce a scheme to be administered through local authorities for rationing the supply of coal to domestic and small industrial consumers and the consumption of gas and electricity by those consumers and that when the Order was made by the Goverment a local fuel overseer would have to be appointed to administer the same on behalf of the local authority, and also that it would be the duty of such authority to provide him with the necessary staff and accommodation. It would further be necessary in the near future to appoint an advisory committee representative of coal, gas and electricity interests in the district (including the Co-operative Societies) for the purpose of advising the overseer on any matter referred to the committee by him. The Borough Treasurer (Mr. J. H. Lindley) was appointed fuel overseer. The appointment of an advistory committee was left over.

The Town Clerk submitted a letter from the Ministry of Health, in which they stated that in view of the passing of the Emergency Powers (Defence) Act it was now proposed to deal with the question of billeting by regulations and reported that the power of appointing billeting officers and a tribunal (consisting of a chairman and two other members) to hear complaints was delegated to the Mayor from lists prepared by the local authority. It was resolved that the following lists be made:—

Billeting officers list, Mr. I. C. Pharaoh, Director of Education, Mr. R. Brooks, Mr. H. Hampson. Tribunal list, The Mayor, Councs. Blackshaw, Morgan, and Bamford, Nurse Belyea.

The thanks of the Council were accorded to the chief officials and their staffs for the services rendered by them in connexion with air raid precautions.

ALL HANDS ON DECK

Woman and children filling sandbags to provide protection for some of the shop cellars which are to be used as air raid shelters.

Decontamination

This service is under the control of the cleansing superintendent, Mr. J. W. Lowe, and is situated at the Destructor Works yard in Twist-lane. The personnel consists of five permanent squads together with reserves. These squads are now on duty 24 hours to the day and at a signal will proceed to any place in the town which might be affected by an air raid. They are equipped with special protective clothing and apparatus necessary to decontaminate buildings or persons.

Cleansing

Construction of a permanent cleansing depot at the Destructor Works in Twist-lane, is in progress and the work will be expedited. Until completion the cleansing depot has been established at the Public Baths in Silk-st., Leigh. Here again there is a trained personel available for the cleansing of persons contaminated with gas.

Auxiliary Fire Services

In addition to the Central Fire Station, auxiliary stations have been established at The Firs, Butts corn mill, and the Parsonage Farm, Westleigh, and a watching post at Pennington. All auxiliary firemen have been called up on permanent duty for the purpose of manning these stations. Firemen are patrolling the streets, everyone of which will be surveyed every eight minutes in an emergency.

Ambulances and First-Aid

First-aid posts are at Bedford Church Crypt, Stone House Clinic and St. John's C.E. School. First-aid parties are based on these posts and also at the Firs Maternity Home. There is also a mobile unit based at The Firs, which is available for casualties in the borough area and also in Abram and Astley. The total number of first-aid parties is 15. The casualty clearing station is at the Infirmary. Ambulances are constantly attached to the first-aid party depots and are available for their normal work from those centres. The ambulance service, which up to the outbreak of war was in charge of the Fire Brigade, is now in charge of the Medical Officer of Health.

In view of the fact that Stone House clinic is being used as a first-aid post the medical services there are in abeyance for the time being. Milk, dried milk and other products are being distributed from the Health Department at the Town Hall. Other Infant Welfare centres will be available as usual for the distribution of dried milk etc

Repair of Roads

Five squads of specially trained and equipped men are permanently standing by at the Destructor Works yard, Twist-lane, Leigh, ready at a moment's notice to proceed to any affected area.

Public Shelters

Public cellar shelters are available at the following places:—Eagle and Child Hotel, Twist-lane (70 persons); Lilford Hotel, Bradshawgate (70); Bull's Head Hotel, Bradshawgate (80); Lord Nelson Hotel, Bradshawgate (70); Rope and Anchor Hotel, Turnpike (100); Boar's Head, Market Place (30); Pied Bull Hotel, Leigh-rd. (80); Courts Hotel, Church-st. (60); White Horse Hotel, Railway-rd. (100); Old Town Hall, King-st. (40); Railway Inn, St. Helens-rd. (30); Boydells, grocers, 276, St. Helens-rd. (20); St. Peter's Vicarage, Firs-lane (60); Fleece Hotel, Market-st. (20); Travellers' Rest, Market-st. (30); Catholic Club, Bold-st. (60); Eagle and Hawk Hotel, Chapel-st. (70); Standard Mower Hotel, Chapel-st. (50). In addition public surface shelters are being built in Chapel-st., Trafalgar-st., each for 100 persons; Manchester-rd. and Holden-rd. (50); Leigh-rd. Kirkhall-lane (100); Marsh Playing Fields, Wigan-rd. (100); Pickley Green, off Westleigh-lane (100).

In due course other cellars will be brought into use as public shelters.

Responsible persons of suitable character and personality are urgently required for the regulation and control of persons within the shelters.

In May last an estimate was made, based on information already in possession of the Town Council of the number of houses in the borough which came within the scheme for the distribution of "Anderson" type shelters was forwarded to the Home Office. The estimated number required was 12,266. Since this estimate was made instructions have been received to make a census of persons entitled to receive a shelter, and this is in progress, and will be completed within the next few days. Persons should not make application for these shelters as they will be delivered by the Railway Co. as soon as they are received.

SAFETY ON THE ROADS

A new service for motorists was provided this week by local firms. Bumpers and steps are whitened to help distinguish them on the darkened roads.

A MOMENTOUS DAY

LEIGH M.P. AND HOUSE OF COMMONS SCENE

I feel that the people of Leigh constituency would desire to have a brief description of what happened in the Houses of Parliament on Sunday, September 3rd, writes Mr. J. J. Tinker, M.P.

On Saturday night, after hearing the Prime Minister's statement on the international situation, the Members were in a disturbed state of mind because there seemed to be some misunderstanding between France and Britain, and we were waiting anxiously for the Prime Minister's speech to be made when we met at 12 o'clock the next day.

I arrived at the House at 10 o'clock and was informed that the Prime Minister would broadcast from Downing-st. at 11-15 and that Members of Parliament would hear it at Committee Room No. 11. We then heard that at 11 o'clock that morning the ultimatum had been made and a state of war now existed with Germany.

We assembled in the Chamber in the House of Commons at 11-30 and immediately we got there the sirens gave out the warning that enemy aircraft were coming, and we must take shelter—a quick reminder that war had come.

At 12 o'clock—noon—the Prime Minister entered and made his promised statement to the Members of the Commons. I have never heard him to be more clear and definite and as he neared the end he was filled with emotion and his concluding words will live long in my memory. He said: "This is a sad day for all

MR. J. J. TINKER, M.P.

of us—and to none is it sadder than to me. Everything I have worked for, everything I have hoped for, everything I believed in during my public life, has crashed to ruins. There is only one thing left for me to do—that is to devote what strength and powers I have to forwarding the victory of the cause for which we have to sacrifice so much."

He was followed by Mr. Greenwood (Deputy Leader of the Opposition) and Sir A. Sinclair (Leader of the Liberal party), and also by Mr. Winston Churchill and Mr. Lloyd George. All four speeches were on similar lines to the Prime Minister. All our efforts to an honourable peace had failed and we were in honour bound to play our part and go to the assistance of Poland.

Sad and serious was the mood of the House of Commons. Many of the Members remembered the experience of the last war but we all felt that no other course could be followed. We had made a pledge—our co-partners to that pledge had been deliberately assailed—and as we would have expected of them to come to our aid, had we been attacked, so we must give all the assistance we can to them.

There was a grim determination to do what we believed is right and just in the cause of liberty and freedom and against oppression of nations, and it was in this spirit we concluded this most momentous sitting of Parliament.

I think we have spoken for the whole of the British people and I am confident everyone of us will do all that lies in his power to win a just peace.

AIR RAID WARNING SIGNALS

Warning of an impending air raid will be given by a fluctuating or "warbling" signal of varying pitch or a succession of intermittent blasts sounded by hooters and sirens.

These signals may be supplemented by sharp blasts on police whistles.

The "raiders' passed" signal will be a continuous signal at a steady pitch.

If poison gas has been used warning will be given by hand rattles.

The ringing of hand bells will announce that the danger from gas has passed.

No Council Elections?

At a special meeting of the Leigh Liberal Association on Monday, Mr. R. Parr, presiding, the following resolution was passed unanimously: "The Leigh Liberal Municipal Association are of the opinion that in times such as the present all parties should sink political differences, and this Association will take no action to change the present constitution of our local Council."

Copies of the resolution have been forwarded to the Conservative and Labour agents.

Schools To Remain Closed

Schools in Leigh have been closed this week and will remain closed the whole of next week. Details of re-opening will be given in the "Journal" as soon as the necessary information has been received.

Day Meetings

Food Control Committee at Golborne

Golborne Council at their monthly meeting on Monday evening were the first local Council to make reference to the outbreak of war.

Counc. E. Prescott, J.P., chairman, said he would like to say how sorry they all were that since their last meeting they had been forced into a war. "You will agree with me," he said, "that every member of this Council will do everything in his power to protect the inhabitants of the area, especially women and children, whilst this terrible conflict lasts." All knew that this country was in the right, and he hoped they would be successful in the end.

At the close of the meeting, Ald. Barrow suggested that in view of the international situation, and the subsequent black-outs, the meetings should be held during the day time. Members would not have to travel unnecessarily in the dark, without lights.

The resolution was seconded by Counc. Oughton, and on the motion of Counc. Naylor it was decided to fix the time of the meetings at 3-0 p.m. on Wednesday.

A special meeting was held after the meeting proper, and a local food control committee was appointed.

The Report Centre

The operation of the whole of the A.R.P. scheme is based in a central control, established in the basement of the Town Hall. Here officers responsible for the various services will be represented. This department, known as the Report Centre, will receive through the medium of the air raid warning services and the police, reports of any injury to property or persons which might take place during an air raid. It will at once be able to send the assistance required. In addition, the centre is in communication with the remainder of the county, so that if required A.R.P. services of other towns may be called upon to assist the services in Leigh. Likewise the Leigh services will be at the call of other authorities if circumstances arise.

Air Raid Wardens

This service, for which the police are responsible, will pass on to the public information as to air raids by means of whistles and hand-rattles or by word of mouth. Posts have been arranged at the following places: Baptist School, Smallbrook-lane; Westleigh Farm, Pickley Green; Red Lion Hotel, Westleigh-lane; 145, Kirkhall-lane; Whittakers, Office, 299, Back Charles-st.; Recreation Room, Brickworks, Wigan-rd.; Livesey's Farm, Wigan-rd.; Sportsman Hotel, Firs-lane; 281, Firs-lane; 73, Leigh-rd.; 40, Back Holden-rd.; 19, Sefton-st.; 142, Holden-rd.; Beechwood, off Holden-rd.; Boundary Hotel, Manchester-rd.; 183, Chapel-st.; 7a, Leigh-rd.; 94, Railway-rd.; Stable, Back Market-st.; Garage, Unionist Rooms, Cook-st.; 35, Gas-st.; 107, Chapel-st.; Bedford Conservative Club, Chapel-st., Ellesmere Hotel, St. Helens-rd.; Robin Hood Farm, St. Helens-rd.; Briarfield, Beech-grove, off St. Helens-rd.; Pennington Hotel, Pennington-rd.; Prospect House, Warrington-rd.; Greyhound Inn, Warrington-rd.

Gas, Electricity and Water

The public utility undertakings owned by the Corporation, gas, electricity, and water, have each organized their A.R.P. so as to cause as little interference as possible with the ordinary services.

The personnel of all A.R.P. activities are standing by 24 hours to the day.

Leigh Town Council has considered a circular from the Ministry of Health as to orders made under the Military Training Act, 1939, and the Reserve and Auxiliary Forces Act, 1939, for the protection of the civil liabilities of persons called out for service under these Acts and in particular to the provision made for the postponement of the repayment of advances made by Building Societies which fall due during such periods of service. The circular states that this procedure might be followed in the case of loans under the Small Dwellings Acquisition Acts in which a postponement of instalments can be permitted without infringing the maximum period of 30 years. It was decided to authorize the Small Dwellings Acquisition Acts Sub-Committee to deal with each case on its merits.

Officers and servants of the Town Council called out for service under the Reserve and Auxiliary Forces Act, 1939, will be allowed for the whole period of absence, the balance of civil pay, so as to bring up their total emoluments, service, and civil, to the level of civil pay.

Basement Shelters

Twenty-two public shelters in basements with accommodation for 1,246 persons are to be constructed as follows: 28, Market-st. (16 persons), 24, Market-st. (37 persons), 5a, 5, and 7, Lord-st. (70 persons), Bridge Inn, St. Helens-rd. (47 persons), 5 and 7, Bradshawgate (71 persons), 71, 73, and 75, Bradshawgate (70 persons), 115, Bradshawgate (29 persons), 14, Bradshawgate (21 persons), 26 and 28, Bradshawgate (21 persons), 30, Bradshawgate (50 persons), 36a, Bradshawgate (18 persons), 38, Bradshawgate (30 persons), 48, Bradshawgate (28 persons), 62, Bradshawgate (28 persons), 76-86, Bradshawgate (174 persons), 96, Bradshawgate (28 persons), 43, Chapel-st. (34 persons), 40, Chapel-st. (30 persons), 100, Chapel-st. (35 persons), Foundry Arms, Chapel-st. (34 persons), Technical School (330 persons), Firs-lane Conservative Club (46 persons).

Leigh is well organized as regards A.R.P.

In the event of an air raid people should remain indoors or if on the street take cover in one of the many shelters provided, and not remain on the streets.

Gas masks should be carried whenever a person leaves the house.

Page four of *Leigh Journal* for 8 September 1939 announcing details of local war preparations.

The mayor, George Holden (sitting in boat no.3), inaugurating the boating lake at Firs Park, 1921.

A Parade to mark the beginning of Leigh, Atherton and Tyldesley Warship Week, 21 March 1942.
Capt R. P. Galer, R.N.R. was on the platform to take the salute at the march past in Market
Square. The Mayor (Cllr Peter Gibson) who was acting as chairman was also in attendance. In
front of the platform was a large cut out model of H.M.S. *Ulysses* (decorated with flags and
pennants), the ship sponsored by the three towns. After the speeches there was a march past of
Army, Navy and Air Force Units headed by the Manchester Home Guard Band with the Leigh
Squadron of the A.T.C. and bugle band also taking part.

On 20 July 1940, Mr J. J. Tinker, Leigh's MP inspected a guard of honour of the local L.D.V. in Ellesmere Street. Afterwards he inspected L.D.V. headquarters, then together with Battalion Commander R. R. Irving he toured road blocks and block houses in the area.

In November 1920 Cllr George Holden was installed as Mayor in the customary mayor-making ceremony in the Council Chamber at Leigh Town Hall. The photograph shows, left to right: Mr T. Bamber (Town Clerk), Cllr George and Mrs Holden (Mayor and Mayoress), Mrs Grundy and William Grundy (ex-Mayor).

Freedom of the Borough: on 2 November 1972 in Leigh Town Hall, Charles Henry Bratt and Thomas Hourigan were each presented with a silver casket and illuminated scroll, to commemorate their admission as honorary freemen. The photograph shows, left to right: Cllr A. Shepherd, Ald. T. Hourigan, Mrs H. J. Davies (Mayoress), Ald. H. J. Davies (Mayor), Ald. C. H. Bratt and Cllr H. Davies and standing behind the Mayor and Mayoress C. Sarginson (Town Clerk). Mr Bratt was the first Labour Councillor to be awarded this honour.

Peter Fazackerley was installed as the 62nd and last Mayor of Leigh in May 1973. Born in Hatton Fold, Atherton he began work in Carrington Mills as an office boy, and subsequently joined Lancashire United Transport, where he worked for 48 years. Under local government re-organisation Leigh Council ceased to exist from April 1974 and became part of the new Wigan Metropolitan Borough. Peter Fazackerley died on 22 April 1984 and was cremated after a service at Kingsleigh Methodist Church.

two

Local
Services

Left: Sgt Hodkinson of the Lancashire Constabulary on a horse hired from Monks' Stables, Leigh, *c*.1908.

Below: A horse-drawn fire engine owned by Hindley Urban District Council. The crown would suggest a royal occasion probably during the early 1900s.

Opposite above: The Lancashire coalfield in April 1912 was the setting for a bitter miners' strike. Fears of serious disorder in the district led the authorities to draft 50 mounted police and about 100 extra constables besides 630 Royal Fusiliers with fixed bayonets and 120 Lancers. The photograph shows 50 mounted police who were billeted at Leigh Fire Station. They were drafted mainly from the Liverpool area.

Opposite below: In June 1922, a large crowd was attracted to a novel ceremony in the Butts area of Leigh. Here they witnessed the christening of a new fire engine by the name of 'Wright' (after Cllr J. H. Wright, Chairman of the Watch Committee). During the ceremony the Mayoress (Mrs G. Holden) broke a bottle of champagne over the engine.

On 30 April 1906 there was a large crowd to see the Mayor (Ald. W. J. Smith JP) open St Mary's Gordens in Gorden Street, Leigh. Canon Irton Smith, Vicar of Leigh moved a vote of thanks.

A corner of Pennington Hall grounds photographed c.1960.

Church Street Gardens, Leigh

Church Street Gardens were opened to the public on 1 June 1901, although the bandstand was still to be erected. This was formally handed over to the corporation at a ceremony on 1 June 1902. It remained on this site until 1921 when it was demolished to make way for the present War Memorial.

Nurses at the Stone House Welfare Centre in June 1921; the baby's weight is being read and recorded. On the first visit of mother and child to the clinic, they were seen by the medical officer who was on hand to give advice and hints. Dried milk and Virol were distributed to the more needy cases.

District Nurse Cull with her cycle and kit bag, c.1910. She worked in the Leigh and Westhoughton areas.

TO THE
PHILANTHROPISTS OF LEIGH PARISH
A PLEA FOR
PUBLIC BATHS.

MAN is a compound of essences--earth, air, fire, and water; and in order to keep the vital machine in perfect working order, a continuous and adequate supply of those essences is necessary. Earth and fire he may have if he can get the necessary means to procure suitable food, and eat it. Air he may get if he will open his door wide, and let in its pure and health-giving qualities. But a perfect external application of God's pure balm-giving water cannot be got by the majority of the inhabitants of Leigh parish. Anyone wishing for a good wash and swim must transport himself to the nearest seaport. Messrs. Isherwood and Hayes's mill, and its continuous supply of water, seem inviting philanthropists to turn to the best possible advantage its natural facilities; and so long as that mill shall be worked these objects may be easily attained. As far as my knowledge of excavation goes, the land adjoining actually seems standing in readiness to be turned to account. Dig out and protect from rough winds these two baths, and you have the stream of pure water passing along to supply one bath with cold, and the engine would supply the other with warm water. So far as the plan is concerned, the work is done with a little outlay; all that is wanted is money. Can a plan be originated by the parties to whom this appeal is made to bring about so desirable an object?

THOMAS HALLIWELL, PRINTER, POST OFFICE, MARKET STREET, LEIGH.

Poster produced by local printer Thomas Halliwell pleading for public baths to be built, *c.*1860. Halliwell founded the *Leigh Chronicle* and was postmaster from 1853 to 1860, when the discovery of his fraud at the Post Office caused him to flee to Belgium.

Leigh's Public Baths in Silk Street was built at a cost of £6,000 and opened by Richard Greenough in 1881. Further extended in 1927 it finally closed in 1977. The original bath was designed by local architect J. C. Prestwich who also designed the Town Hall. This view shows the entrance to the Turkish Baths, opened in 1902.

Leigh Library staff at work in the mid 1930s. The young man stamping a book on the left of the picture is James Blackburn who eventually became Borough Librarian.

An advance in local library provision was seen in 1924, when a separate lending library and reading room specifically for children was opened. The room situated below the main Reference Department had space for about sixty children.

During the 1926 General Strike a soup kitchen for needy children was opened at Brunswick School, Leigh Road, Hindley Green.

'Who do you think you're kidding Mr Hitler?' A group of Local Defence Volunteers (later renamed the Home Guard) from 'B' Company outside Pennington Hall in the early 1940s.

Something old and something new in Leigh Civic Square. The obelisk flaunts its old age in front of the new Leigh Library which was officially opened by the Rt. Hon. Lord Maybray-King, on 3 November 1971. It is now known as the Turnpike Centre.

A 'Knocker Up' at work. Here he can be seen 'rousting' someone in the Old Weavers Cottages, Twist Lane, around 1930.

Above: The new telephone exchange switchboard which was opened in November 1925 near the Post Office. The old exchange had been in Henrietta Street. It was equipped for 700 lines with an ultimate capacity for 2,000. On the extreme right is Mr E. G. Wallis, Leigh's Post Master.

Below: Visitors inspecting the imposing power house on the ground floor of the new telephone exchange. Cllr W. Higgenbottom (third from right) took a keen interest in the working of the exchange.

Leigh Telegraph Boys in uniform sometime before 1914.

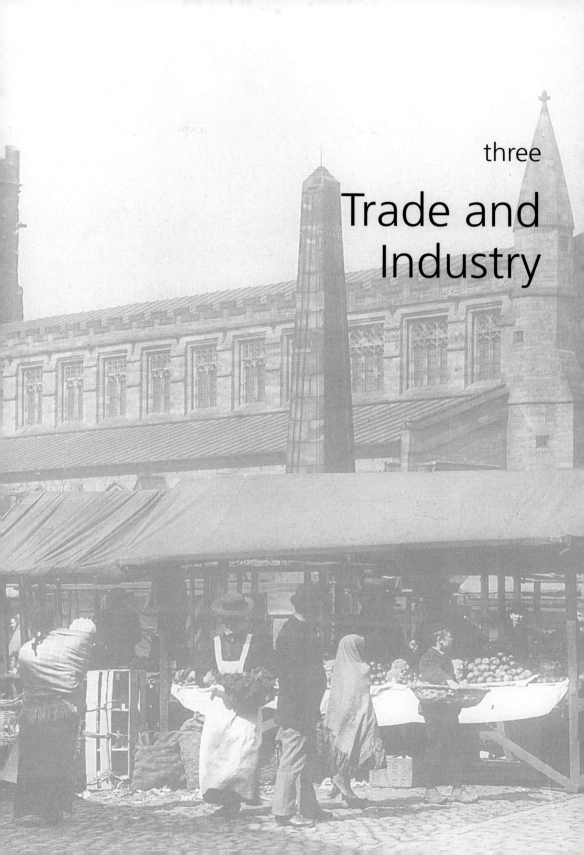

three

Trade and Industry

This view of the old Leigh Market was taken sometime before April 1902 when the new clock at the parish church was installed.

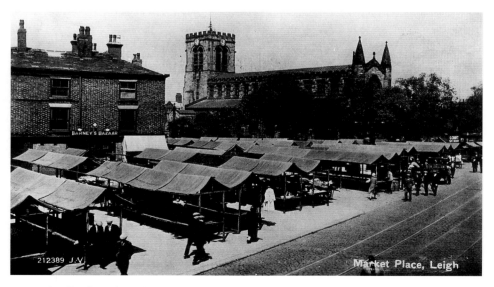

Covered stalls of Leigh Market on its original site, c.1930. The market was normally open for business on Wednesday mornings, Friday and Saturday. Barney's Bazaar, a famous local emporium, is shown behind the stalls.

A rare view of a thriving Leigh Market from the tower of the parish church in the early 1960s. The buildings in the centre of the photograph were demolished to make way for the new Civic Square and Leigh Library.

A day to remember for local residents and traders. On 30 March 1968 the market opened its stalls for the last time before being moved to the new site and indoor market hall north of the parish church.

Bob Rudd, Chairman of the Leigh Market
Trader's Association behind his stall shortly
before moving to the indoor market hall
in 1968.

Albert Green at work behind his
fish stall on Leigh Market in the
1960s. He was also known as the
'Son of Fish Lil'.

Right: 'Never mind the quality feel the width!' Hilda's stall on the old outdoor Leigh Market, with Mrs Hilda Jones and husband examining the towels.

Below: The south side of the Market Place, Leigh, shortly before demolition at the turn of the century. To the left of the picture is McClellan's outfitting shop at 5 Market Place. Henry Fletcher's shop is No.10. Fletcher had been listed as tool and shoemaker since the mid 1850s. The site was cleared for the new Town Hall.

In October 1952, 120 Leigh and district tradesmen, shopkeepers, local government officials and sweet manufacturers together with their wives were photographed on a visit to Cadbury's at Bournville. They travelled by special train, and returned with mementos of cocoa and biscuits.

Above: A view of the old cobbled Market Street, looking north into Market Place around 1899. Centre right is Henry Shovelton's Bedding Warehouse at No.5. At No.7 could be found his grocers shop. At far right at No.17 Thomas Youd's shop is advertising table water in syphons.

Opposite above: In August 1907 Leigh Co-operative Society celebrated its jubilee. There was a procession of employees and delegates from other societies. Prizes were awarded for the best groomed horses and best displays. The Drapery Department seen here was awarded first prize for the best display of goods and second prize for the best turnout. Prize money amounted to 25s 0d and 15s 0d, respectively.

Opposite below: Leigh Co-operative Friendly Society opened a branch in Atherton Road, Hindley Green, in February 1878. Here the five employees pose outside the shop, *c*.1910.

Left: Walter Seddon's drapery shop could be found at 15 Leigh Road. His window display was photographed in the early 1900s.

Opposite above: Collier's 'Duva' Bakery in Leigh was established by William Collier JP in the late 1890s. This horse-drawn van proclaims that William Collier became champion baker in September 1912, a title gained at the International Bakers' and Confectioners' Exhibition at the Agricultural Hall, London. He was awarded the National Association's 60 guinea challenge cup and £100 in cash for the best loaves, one cottage, one tin.

Below: Teofolo Manfredi emigrated to England in the early 1890s with his wife and family. By the early 1920s the Manfredis had established an ice cream business in Leigh. Here Dominic (3rd from left) and Joseph Serventi (4th from left) are photographed with four of the horse-drawn ice cream carts at the bottom of Brown Street, Bedford. Ted Hudson, the man on the far left eventually emigrated to Australia.

Advert for Boardman's furniture shop at 16, Railway Road, Leigh, 1930.

The Leigh Chamber of Trade's Autumn Shopping Festival in 1929 was held from 29 November to 14 December. Posing in front of a decorated bus advertising the event are, from left to right: Messes J. Crawford, E. Davidson, T. Brantwood, P. Boydell, T. E. Ince (Hon. Sec.), F. Daven-port and C. Owen.

Opposite: A group of shopworkers outside Ratcliffe's hardware shop in Bradshawgate, *c*.1950.

A typical turn of the century corner shop at Newton Street. At the far right is the entrance to Sugar Street and beyond that the Savings Bank.

Leach's newsagents shop and the former Regal Cinema, c.1980. All the property here was demolished to make way for Leigh's new bus station (opened 9 February 1992) and Spinning Jenny Way. Above the Spinning Jenny Street name are the Spinning Jenny mural tiles, placed in the wall in 1911 by the property owner George Olivant JP.

William Brown (1871-1928), last town crier of Leigh from 1921-28. Mr Brown went down the pit at the age of fourteen. He lost his sight at the age of 21, afterwards making cane and rush chairs, and knocking up, commencing his round as a knocker-up at 3.30 in the morning. As town crier he attended by-elections and party-political meetings. He called the news in Leigh Market Place during the General Strike of 1926, when no papers were printed. Unofficially, parents of lost children would ask him to shout for them.

Originally the Millstone Inn was located in Parsonage Lane, Westleigh within the area of Pickley Green called Jacob's Well. At a later date the address became 184, Westleigh Lane. Licensees included: 1825 John Thompson, 1836 Thomas Shovelton, 1895 Benjamin Woolstencroft. This photograph was taken shortly before the building was demolished around 1906. It is also interesting to note that a 'Jacob's Well' was christened on 21 March 1854 in the garden belonging to a John Newton of Atherton Cottage, Warrington Road.

The Shepherds Inn, Newton Road was known as 'Th'owd Terminus' because the trams originally only ran to the Leigh–Lowton boundary on which this pub was located. Probably photographed sometime before the 1930s when George Shaw's Brewery was taken over by Peter Walker & Sons.

Rachel Smith of Hesketh Meadow Lane, Lowton, was virtually the last person in the district to spin and weave silk by hand. She died on 22 February 1929 at the ripe old age of ninety-one, having attributed her longevity 'to good thick meal porridge and not so much of your sweet stuff'.

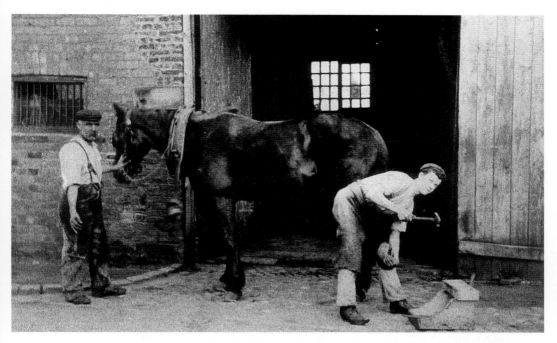

Farrier work being carried out by Mat Hawarth, apprentice to the blacksmith Jethro Higson who is keeping eye on his charge. This photograph was probably taken in the early 1910s before the smithy was demolished to make way for the bungalow at 263 Newton Road.

Some of Boydell's ironworkers with their bicycles in April 1897. The Brown Street Ironworks was founded by William Boydell in 1885 and was finally closed in August 1964.

Richard Greenough,

4-PULL BEER ENGINE.

Strong Quadrant Action, Handsome Moulded
Mahogany or Walnut Case.

ESTIMATES FOR ALL CLASS OF FITTINGS.

TELEPHONES ERECTED AND MAINTAINED.

Anchor Brass Works, Leigh.

Above: A rare photograph of the Anchor Cable Works taken around 1935. The Anchor Cable Co. Ltd., was formed on 31 December 1900 with George Shaw (brewer) as Chairman. In 1903 the company was purchased by Callender's Cable & Construction Co. Ltd., later to become BICC.

Left: An advert for a brass beer engine produced by Richard Greenough jnr's brassfounding works at 38 Bold Street in the nineteenth century.

Opposite above: A group of workers from McGregor Brothers Foundry posed for this photograph in the early 1900s.

Opposite below: Agricultural binding machines from the Albion Ironworks loaded and ready for transportation by rail. The site is probably Leigh Goods Yard in the early 1920s.

A mining landscape which has now completely vanished. Pithead gear at Bickershaw Colliery which was closed in 1992, the last mine in the Leigh district.

The making of reeds for the weaving industry was an unusual but important craft in Leigh. It was pioneered by local Chartist Thomas Howarth of King Street in the early 1800s. His apprentice Robert Leather established his own workshop which remained in the family until closure in 1969. This photograph was taken at Leather's workshop in Mansleys Passage, c.1930.

Barefoot employees at work in Jones' New Cotton Mill, Bedford Square, Leigh, around the turn of the century.

Barges on the Bridgewater Canal heading for the connection with the Leigh branch of the Leeds Liverpool Canal, c.1960. Mather Lane Cotton Mill and bridge can be seen in the background.

STONE DEALERS.

Bibbington Samuel, West Leigh — John Adamson, agent
Fairclough Bros. (& flag & slate), Canal wharf

STONEMASONS.

Chadwick William, Leigh rd
Hughes David (monumental), Silk st
Ranicar Peter (& flagger & monumental mason), Church st
Sinclair John, 19 Queen st
Wright Peter, Silk st. & Union st

STOVE, GRATE & KITCHEN RANGE MANUFACTURERS.

Picksley, Sims & Co. Limited, Bedford Foundry, Leigh, Robert Davison, sec—
T A "Picksleys, Leigh"

SURGEON.

Anderton Charles, M.D. 86 Bradshawgate
Doyle Edward A. M.B. 115 Bradshawgate
Evans George H. M.D. 6 Avenue pl
Hall John, 2 Brown st
Hayes James, 3 Church st
Jones Benjamin, M.D. Bridge st
King James, M.B. 53 Chapel st. Bedford
Perrin John Beswick, 88 Bond st
Sephton Richard, M.D. Springfield, Culcheth

SURVEYORS.

Banks, Fairclough & Stephen (land, mining & engineering), Church st. & 60 King st. Manchester
Prestwich James C. Brown st
Smith John, Etherstone Hall, Pennington
Travers T. W. (land surveyor, mining engineer, land agent, valuer, &c.), Bank chambers, King street

TAILORS.

Marked thus * are also Drapers.

*Buckley James, 2 King st
*Crawshaw Samuel, 26 Queen st. Bedford
Dakin Thomas, 66 Plank la. West Leigh
Galvin William, 43 King st
Hatfield William, 69 Chapel st. Bedford
Kirkman John, 6 Newton st
Leigh Friendly Co-operative Society, Lmtd. 61 Ellesmere st. & branches—Thos. Boydell, sec
M'Lellan Samuel, 5 & 6 Market pl
Okell & Sons, 18 Bradshawgate, & at Tyldesley
O'Neill Michael, 114 Chapel st. Bedford
*Prescot James, 25 Chapel st
*Reid William, 13 Market st
Roberts Edward, Astley
*Shovelton Emanuel, 9 Market st
Simister Timothy, 71 Bradshawgate
Towers Lovell, 468 Leigh rd
Waterfield Samuel, 96 Bradshawgate
*Williams James, 58 Bradshawgate
Yates Thomas T. 11 Chapel st. Bedford

TAVERNS & PUBLIC HOUSES.

Black Horse, Geo. Berry, 58 Chapel st. Bedford
Boar's Head, William Prescott, 2 Market pl
Boat House, Thomas Unsworth, Astley
Bowling Green, John Hulmes, Abram, West Leigh
Bowling Green, Peter Prescott, Leigh rd
Bowling Green, Frederick Green, Green Lane end, Bedford
Bowling Green, William Fairclough, 416 Wigan rd. West Leigh
Britannia, Peter Welsby, Abram, West Leigh
Brown Cow, William Rowson, 19 Bridge st
Brunswick, Wm. Cocker, 70 Chapel st. Bedford
Bull & Butcher, Thos. Prescott, Dangerous corner, West Leigh
Bull's Head, John Halliwell, Butts bridge, Bedford
Bull's Head, Samuel Partington, Astley
Bull's Head, Sarah Ann Makin, 18 & 20 Bradshawgate
Canteen, James Walsh, Astley
Cart & Horses, Richard Cooke, Astley
Chat Moss, Robert Valentine, Glazebury
Church, Francis Parr, 478 West Leigh la. West Leigh
Commercial, Sarah Prescott, Manchester rd. Bedford [Leigh
Correction Inn, Wm. Wallis, Plank la. West
Crown, William Prescott, 7 Hope st
Eagle & Child, Joseph Barker, 46 King st
Ellesmere, Wm. Sharples, 20 St. Helens rd. Pennington
Fir Tree, Jas. Hurst, 170 Firs la. West Leigh
Fleece, William Eden, 31 Market st

Fox, Thomas Wilkinson, 15 Market pl
George & Dragon, Mary Ann Beech, Glazebury
Golden Fleece, Samuel Part, Astley
Greyhound, John Stout, Glazebury, Culcheth
Harrow, Ellen Welsby, Newchurch, Culcheth
King's Head, James E. Mansley, 16 Market pl
Lord Nelson, James Pendlebury, 56 Bradshawgate [West Leigh
Millstone, Wm. Parkinson, West Leigh la.
New Inn, John Dean, 235 Firs la. West Leigh
Pack Horse, Ann Lowe, Newchurch, Culcheth
Pied Bull, Hannah Taylor, 15 Bridge st
Queen's Arms, Ann Wyatt, 1 Market st
Railway, Joseph Glover, 200 Twist la. West Leigh
Raven, John Rigby, Glazebury
Red Lion, Saml. H. Greenhalgh, West Leigh la. West Leigh
Royal Oak, Peter Radcliffe, 54 King st
Saddle, Edward Worthington, 7 Market pl
Sportsman, Margaret Drinkwater, 1 Firs la. West Leigh
Swan, Henry Cross, 9 Bridge st
Swan, Henry Harrison, Astley
Swan, William Drew, 1 Bridge st [st
Walmsley Arms, Edmund Seddon, 22 Market
Wheat Sheaf, Robert Wilcock, Butts bridge, Bedford

RETAILERS OF BEER.

Adamson John, 76 West Leigh la. West Leigh
Allred James, 70 King st
Arkwright William, 87 Bradshawgate
Ashton Thomas, Glazebury
Atkinson James, Kirkhall la
Ball Richard, 28 Vernon st
Bandy James, Glazebury
Banks John, 9 Brown st
Battersby Joseph, 211 Wigan rd. West Leigh
Baxter Ellen, Mather la. Bedford
Bennett Luke, 328 Leigh rd
Booth Jane, 22 Queen st. Bedford
Bowden Harriet, 36 Bradshawgate
Bowden James, 105 Bradshawgate
Brown Peter, Astley
Carter John, 96 Chapel st. Bedford
Chadwick Ellen, 200 Chapel st. Bedford
Coward Wm. 33 St. Helens rd. Pennington
Crank Thomas, Pickley Green, West Leigh
Crank William, 378 Chapel st. Bedford
Critchley Richard, 240 West Leigh la. West Leigh
Dootson Albert R. 55 Chapel st. Bedford
Downing Matthew, 1 Twist la
Fell Betty, Firs la. West Leigh
Fort Robert, 21 & 28 Bradshawgate
Frost James, 28 Firs la. West Leigh
Green Edward, 349 Wigan rd. West Leigh
Green Richard, 15 & 17 Lord st
Gregory James, 95 Chapel st. Bedford
Grundy David, Astley
Grundy James, Heath la. West Leigh
Guest Thomas, 87 Manchester rd. Bedford
Halford Robert, 33 King st
Hatton Henry, 73 Bradshawgate
Hayes James, 92 Abram, West Leigh
Higham Thos. 61 West Leigh la. West Leigh
Hill James, Pennington
Hill William, 18 Market pl
Hodson Thomas, 10 Brown st
Holland Joseph, Astley
Holliday Thomas, 20 & 22 Union st
Howard John, 68 Kirkhall la
Hurst Robert, 77 West Leigh la. West Leigh
Hurst William, 180 Chapel st. Bedford
Isherwood James, 106 Twist la
Johnson Gerrard, 150 Chapel st. Bedford
Kendrick Joseph, 16 Nel Pan la. West Leigh
Kershaw Mary A. Glazebury, Culcheth
Knowles James, 260 Chapel st. Bedford
Latham Robert, 44 St. Helens rd. Pennington
Leigh William, Glazebury, Culcheth
Lonsdale William, 122 Chapel st. Bedford
Lowe Alice, Newchurch
Lowe John, Kirkhall la
Makin John Edward, 90 Chapel st. Bedford
Marsh James, Glazebury
Meadows John, 43 Small Brook la. West Leigh
Merrick James, Culcheth
Naylor Joseph, 277 Plank la. West Leigh
Newton William, Astley
O'Neil James, 2 Queen st
Parr Thomas, 91 Kirkhall la
Prescott Wright, 23 Duke st. Bedford
Ratcliffe Richard, 133 West Leigh la. West Leigh [Leigh
Rothwell Catherine, 168 Wigan rd. West
Seddon Edmund, 138 & 140 Bradshawgate
Shovelton Thomas, 33 Chapel st. Bedford
Shuttleworth James, 286 Chapel st. Bedford
Smith Paul, 192 Plank la. West Leigh
Smith Thomas, 23 Plank la. West Leigh
Southern James, 8 Welsh hill, Twist la
Southern Matthew, 47 Dukinfield st. Bedford
Tobin James, 7 St. Helens rd. Pennington
Turner John T. West Leigh la. West Leigh

Unsworth Thomas, Newchurch, Culcheth
Wallace Henry, 66 King st
Walton Robert, Marsland Green, Astley
Whittaker Peter, 107 Bradshawgate
Wilcock William, Marsland Green, Astley
Wild James, 97 West Leigh la. West Leigh
Wilkinson Geo. 17 College st. Bedford
Wilkinson Sarah, 56 Chapel st. Bedford
Winstanley Elizabeth, 222 Chapel st. Bedford
Worden William, Glazebury
Wright John, Newchurch, Culcheth
Wyatt John, 25 Market st
Yates James, 153 Chapel st. Bedford
Yates Ellen, 60 & 62 Chapel st. Bedford
Yates Robert, 78 Chapel st. Bedford
Yates Thomas, Astley

TELEPHONE COMPANY.

Lancashire & Cheshire Telephonic Exchange Co. Limited, head office, 38 Faulkner st. Manchester
—See advertisement opposite Telephone Company in Manchester Trades List

TIMBER DEALERS.

Cleworth James, Newchurch, Culcheth
Limon Joseph, Queen st. Bedford
Norbury Thomas, Henrietta st
Wright Peter, Lord st & Union st

TOBACCONISTS.

Ackers Charles, 51 Bradshawgate
Beardsworth James E. 50 Bradshawgate
Dawson John, 5 Bradshawgate
Mansley Sarah, 23 King st
Mitchell Frederick M. 67 Chapel st. Bedford
Smith Thomas, 15 Chapel st. Bedford
Williamson James, 79 Bradshawgate
Wolstencroft Edwin, 8 Market st

VETERINARY SURGEONS.

Bennett John W. Courts Hotel yard, Church st
Darwell J. S. & Son, 41 Bradshawgate
Pendlebury James, 56 Bradshawgate

WATCH & CLOCK MAKERS.

Bent Peers, 6 Market st
Clare Hugh, 32 Chapel st. Bedford
Holman William J. 77 Bradshawgate
Johnson Thomas, 108 Bradshawgate
Knowles James, 260 Chapel st. Bedford
O'Connor Timothy, 32 Market st
Parson E. A. 14 King st
Roberts Thomas, 69 Bradshawgate
Tinsley James, 3 Market st
Woolley John (clocks in town or country attended to), 156 Chapel st. Bedford

WHEELWRIGHTS.

Allred James, Old Workhouse yard, King st
Cleworth Ellen, Glazebury, Culcheth
Cleworth James, Newchurch, Culcheth
Fletcher Thomas, College st. Bedford
Gerrard John, Mathers lane, Bedford
Gregory Benjamin, 43 Chapel st. Bedford
Hill William Abram, West Leigh
Smith James, 5 Portland st

WHITESMITHS.

Barnes Eli, Glazebury, Culcheth
Crompton William, 30 Market st
Prescott James, 114 Bradshawgate

WINE & SPIRIT MERCHANTS.

Hargreaves Margaret, 37 Chapel st. Bedford
Shovelton James (exors. of), Hope st
Tomlinson George S. (& ale & porter bottler), 110 Bradshawgate [Bedford
Unsworth John (British wine), 22 Chapel st.

MISCELLANEOUS.

Banks Edwin, music seller, 55 Lord st
Battersby James, furniture remover, Back Salford
Boydell Thomas, secretary to Leigh Co-operative Society, Limited, 41 Church st
Boydell William, washing & wringing machine maker, &c. Brown st
Brogden Thomas, clothes dealer, 65 Chapel st. Bedford [Leigh
Bryce William, cashier, 156 Firs lane, West
Burns Thomas & Allen, candle manufacturers, Lord st [Church st
Charlton James, professor of music, 33
Cleworth Peter, hay dealer, Vicarage square
Collier Mary Ann, market gardener & florist Pennington

A page from Slater's 'Royal National Commercial Directory and the Manufacturing District Around Manchester'. It shows some of the trades and occupations being carried out in 1887.

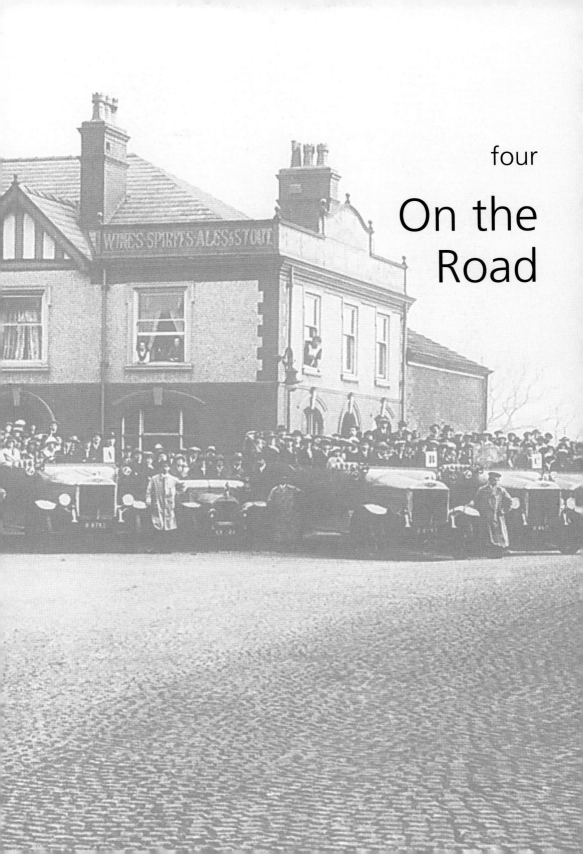

four

On the Road

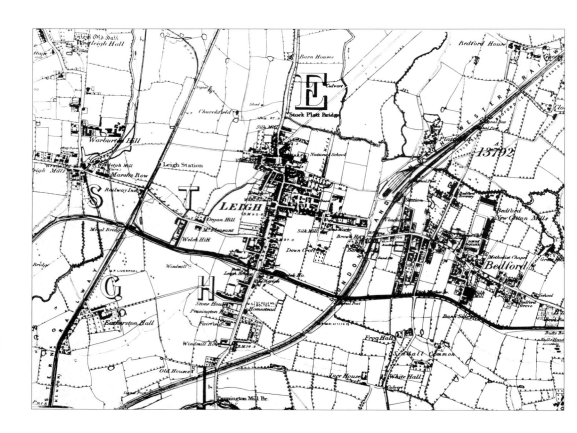

Beech Walk Entrance,
St Helens
Pennington, Leigh

Opposite above: A section of the 6 inch OS map for the area (1849), showing three forms of transport: the Bridgewater and Leigh Branch Canals running east to west, the early railways through the town and the ancient road pattern. Some new streets have been built but Leigh's period of rapid growth was only beginning at this period. The main railway was not opened until 1864 and this was overprinted when the map was reissued.

Opposite below: Open-topped tram passing Beech Walk en route to Lowton along St Helens Road, September 1911.

Right: A September 1902 saw the first trial run of trams in Leigh. Between then and 1933 they operated with great success. Here open–topped tram No.27 travels along King Street.

Below: A group of road workers at the turn of the century in Glazebury.

A group of council workers at Plank Lane in the early 1920s; they seem to be laying water pipes.

A well kept and blooming Pennington Station around the early part of the century. Originally named Bradshaw Leach, it was opened on 11 July 1831, and was renamed in 1877. The station was situated by the entrance to what is now Pennington Flash Country Park, the road past the Flash being originally a railway line.

A rare view of the last steam locomotive stopping at St Mary's Station, Lowton. Opened in 1884, the station was demolished in 1964 following the closure of the branch line.

Leigh Railway Station during its demolition in May 1969. With the closure of the railway Leigh became one of the largest English towns to be deprived of a passenger service.

A party of employees from Carrington Mills, Kirkhall Lane, photographed here in a charabanc in London on their way to the British Empire Exhibition at Wembley, August 1924. They had been driven to Lowton St Mary's Station where they boarded a train for London.

In the early 1920s, the King's Arms, Lane Head, Lowton, was the starting point for this fleet of charabancs, probably preparing for a Bank Holiday outing.

In the early 1900s William Morgan was the proud owner of one of the first motor cars in the area. He was photographed behind the wheel, somewhere near the top of The Avenue in Leigh. Later he became a local auctioneer and in 1936 was elected Mayor. He died in February 1954.

A coal wagon from the Lowton area, 1935. Mr Warburton and Mr H. Eckersley are pictured beside their vehicle.

This 'Dennis' lorry was owned by H. Maudsley of Moss View, Newton Road, Lowton. The picture was taken around 1920.

A collection of vehicles owned by the Borough of Leigh Highways Department probably in the early 1950s.

Opposite below: Monday 31 August 1958 marked the end of an era when the last trolley bus ceased operation. It passed by Leigh Market just as the parish church clock struck twelve. The bus was photographed outside the Atherton Depot.

n 1924, Leigh Corporation Transport Department accepted a tender of £1,250 from Leyland Motors for the supply of this thirty-seater motor omnibus. Tom Parry (far left) was the coach builder.

ORDER OF LOCAL GOVERNMENT BOARD,
20—3—78.

Form B.

London: KNIGHT & CO., 90 Fleet Street.

Register of Canal Boats.

Leigh _____ _Registration Authority._

1. Registration Number of the boat ... **one.**

2. Name of the boat, or if there be no name, the number ... ... **The "Joseph Baker"**

3. Christian Name, Surname, and Address of Owner* ... **James Diggle, Hindley Green Hall near Wigan, Lancashire.**

4. Christian Name and Surname of Master... ... ... **Charles Gerrard.**

5. Route along which the boat is accustomed or intended to ply ... **Leeds and Liverpool Canal, Bridgewater Canal, River Weaver and River Mersey.**

6. Nature of the traffic in which the boat is accustomed or intended to be employed ... **Coal and Salt.**

7. Mode of propulsion; and whether a "wide" or "narrow" boat; and whether to be used as a "fly" boat worked by shifts ... ... **Propelled by horse power a "wide" boat not to be used as a "fly" boat**

8. Number of cabins in the boat ... ... **Two.**

9. Dimensions and cubical capacity of the cabin or cabins :—

Rule of measurement and of deduction adopted :—†

additional to cabin taken out of hold of Boat 5.4 × 2. 10 × 4. 6 = 67.0

Rule A.

After Cabin...		ft.	in.
Height...		4	7
Length		6	9
Width ...		6	2
Gross cubical capacity ...		190	8
Net cubical capacity or free air space		190	8

Fore Cabin ...			
Height...		4	6
Length ...		7	2
Width ...		7	2
Gross cubical capacity		231	"
Net cubical capacity or free air space		231	

* If the boat is owned by a partnership firm, or by a company or association, corporate or unincorporate, state the name of the firm, company, or association, and their principal office or place of business.

† Here state whether Rule A. or Rule B. [See Note to Form (A.) of Examining Officer's Report] has been adopted in the measurement of the cabin or cabins ;—distinguishing, in each case, where necessary, the rate of deduction.

A page from the Register of Canal Boats for 1878 records that the 'Joseph Barker' was intended to carry both coal and salt. James Diggle (who died in May 1880), proprietor of Westleigh Colliery was the registered boat owner.

five

In the
Classroom

The foundation stone of Leigh Technical School and Public Library on Railway Road was laid by the Hon. John Powys on 10 September 1892. The completed building, designed by local architects J. C. Prestwich and J. H. Stephen is seen here being officially opened by Lord Derby on 26 September 1894.

On 31 January 1927 Stephen Walsh (front left) and his wife were received by Ald. H. Speakman (Chairman of the Higher Education Committee) and James Ward (Director of Education) at Leigh Municipal College, to officially open the new mining department. Walsh was elected as MP for Ince division for the newly formed Labour Party in 1906, retaining the seat until his death in 1929. He was a popular man locally, a true working class MP, and achieved Cabinet rank as Secretary of State for War in the short-lived first Labour Government.

Right: Leonard Berger Benny was the Principal of Leigh's Municipal College in the 1920s. Prior to his coming to Leigh, Benny had been lecturer in Mechanics and Mathematics at Goldsmiths College as well as Professor of Mathematics at University College, Exeter.

Below: Leigh's first council school on Windermere Road was opened by the Mayor (Cllr G. Hunter JP) on 25 June 1908. After this photograph was taken by local photographer Wragg, the architect J. C. Prestwich presented the Mayor with a gold key. Prestwich designed many local buildings including the town hall and baths.

The 1918 Education Act ended the half time system of education and established 14 as the uniform compulsory leaving age and also provided for the establishment of continuation schools. These were to provide part-time evening education for leavers. A class of Leigh youngsters is shown here learning multiplication principles to calculate a yearly wage.

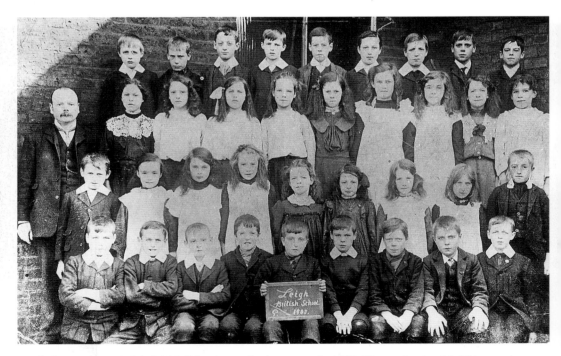

Pupils from a class at Leigh British School pose for the camera in 1905. The teacher is a Mr Thinsworth.

A group of girls from St Thomas' Church School, Bedford, at play, *c*.1910.

To escape the London blitz a group of fourteen- to sixteen-year-old evacuees from Kingston Day
Commercial School, Surrey came to stay with families in Leigh. They were photographed in July 1944.
On 22 April 1995 a reunion of evacuees and host families took place at the Greyhound Hotel, Leigh.
A plaque to commemorate the event can be seen in Leigh Library.

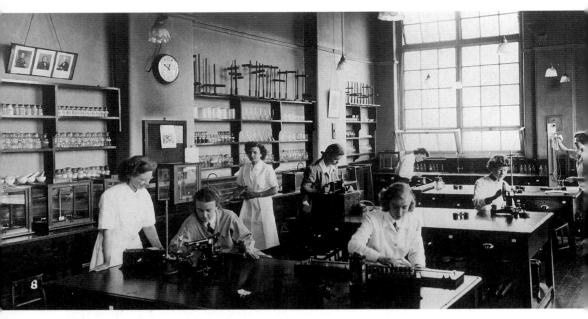

A view of the physics and chemistry laboratory of Leigh Girls Grammar School, July 1951.

A class of Leigh Grammar School girls prepares for exercises in the Marsh Gymnasium sometime in the 1930s.

Opposite below: Pennington House on St Helens Road which had been vacated by the Misses Bowker opened on 24 January 1933 as St Hilda's C. of E. Secondary School. The ceremony was performed by Rev. the Hon. Edward Lyttleton DD (former headmaster of Eton). Also in attendance was the Prioress of Whitby.

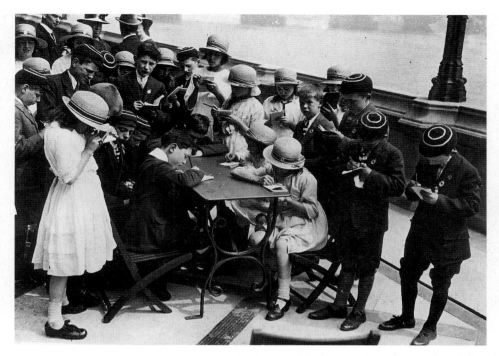

Between 22 and 27 May 1922, a group of children from Leigh Primary Schools went on an educational trip to London. Here they can be seen making notes on the terrace of the House of Commons which they visited on 24 May, which was also Empire Day.

LEIGH GRAMMAR SCHOOL,

LEIGH, NEAR MANCHESTER,

Sept 29th 1882

Mr Travers

To RALPH PASSE, Dr.

TERMS : A quarter's notice in writing, or a quarter's fees, required previous to a pupil's removal. Quarterly payments. No deductions made.

To Master W Travers's Board			
& Tuition for the quarter ended on the above date	7	10	-
Piano Lessons and Piano 2/. Music 1/6	1	2	6
Singing do., &c. Laundress 10/6	"	10	6
Pens, Pencil, &c. 1/ Drawing	"	2	"
3 MSS. Books 9" — Church Props. 18.	-	1	7
Books, &c. :— Cricket	"	2	6
Hair, pomade, amusements	"	1	"
Repairs of windows ...	"	1	6
2 towels 1/2 ; 2 ditto 2/9	"	3	11
Visit to Liverpool &c	"	3	"
Fare to Golborne	-	"	6
Received			
£ o	£9	19	"

Paid 28th 1882

Ralph Passe

Many thanks RP

Above: In January 1932 the Vicar of Leigh cut the first sod for the foundations of the new nursery and infants' school to be built in Vicarage Gardens. Left to right are: Rev. J. E. Eastwood BA (vicar), Rev. C. V. Roberts, Cllr T. Hindley JP (Mayor), M. A. E. Prescott (Builder), Miss Ackers (Headmistress, Infants Dept.), Mr H. Plumb (Headmaster, Leigh C. of E. Boys School), Miss Byrom (Headmistress, Leigh C. of E. Girls Dept.).

Left: An account from headmaster Ralph Passe for the board and education of a Master W. Travers of Golborne 1882. Two items of interest: 1s 0d, pomade and amusements and 1s 6d for repairs to windows.

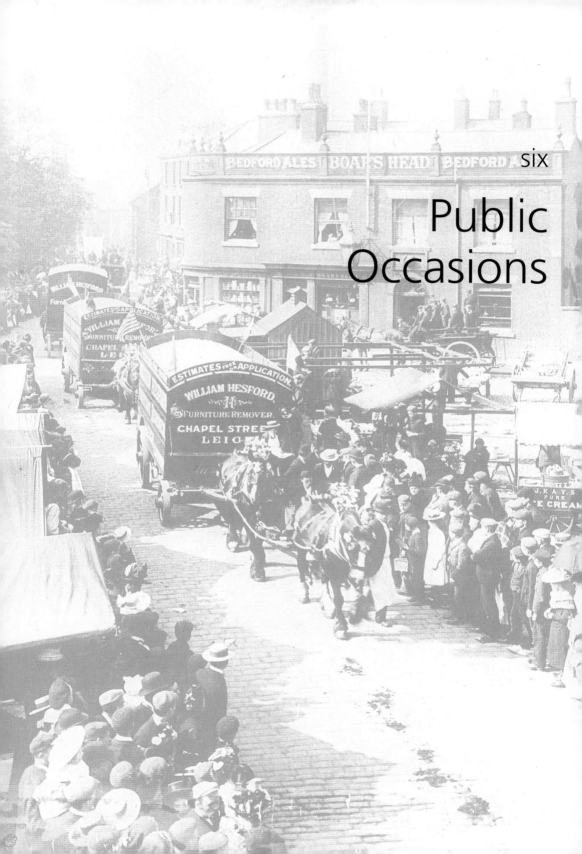

six

Public
Occasions

Above: Between 25 September and 1 October 1949 the Corporation of Leigh held a civic week to commemorate fifty years as a Municipal Borough. There was a full programme of events including this grand pageant and carnival which was held on 1 October.

Left: St Joseph's Roman Catholic Church Walking Day, early 1900s. Saturday, 29 June 1907 was a red letter day in the annals of Leigh Catholicism. This was the first time that the joint congregation of St Joseph's, The Sacred Heart, Twelve Apostles and Our Lady of the Rosary were united in a grand procession.

St John's Church, Hindley Green, Walking Day in 1948. The photograph shows members of the Sunday School on the second of the two days, Sunday 26 June, when over 600 people participated. Thatto Heath Independent Methodist Brass Band and St John's Boy's Brigade Brass Band accompanied the procession.

Abram Colliery Band leading a walking day procession, c.1920. By 1937 the band had changed its name to Bickershaw Colliery Band, by which time it had become one of the finest brass bands in Lancashire.

Above: In 1911 there was a procession at Glazebury with about 900 people taking part. It was headed by Glazebury Prize Band. Other groups included Glazebury Church Sunday School teachers and pupils, and members of the Druid's and Shepherd's Friendly Societies. The photograph shows some of the smaller children who were carried upon five lurries supplied by Messrs J. Johnson, R. Wareing, Henry Johnson, R. Taylor and Paul Taylor. The location is possibly outside Glazebury Vicarage.

Left: Four children with baskets of flowers in a milk cart. The photograph from the early part of this century was taken in Bolton House Road during a Bickershaw Walking Day Procession.

Right: The Lifeboat Saturday Movement in Leigh organised its first demonstration on Saturday 8 May 1896. The aim of the Movement was to raise funds for the Royal National Lifeboat Institution. Part of the procession included these horse–drawn wagons owned by William Hesford. To the left some of the market stalls can be seen.

Below: Pennington Church Walking Day in June 1950. In the procession was the 1950 May Queen (Miss Joan Wilde) and her retinue.

In August 1925, Leigh Friendly Co-operative Society promoted a fancy dress carnival and sports day. It was estimated that over 1,500 persons took part in the procession. A variety of costumes and a wealth of colour and novelty excited the admiration of onlookers. The photographer managed to capture two members of Leigh Borough Brass Band (bottom right) on Market Street. Every child who walked in the procession received a memento. The procession began at the Society's offices in Ellesmere Street and proceeded along Twist Lane, Findlay Street, Windermere Road, Market Street, Bradshawgate to Bedford Square before wending its way to the Athletic Ground.

A gaily decorated heavy horse pulls Leigh Co-operative Society's Flour Mill float during the Jubilee procession of August 1907. Peter Wood of the Corn Mill Department, who decorated the horse won a commendation for his efforts.

Arrowe Park on the Wirral was the venue for the World Boy Scout Jamboree in August 1929. On 8 August a group of Danish scouts from the Jamboree visited Leigh where they were given a civic reception by the Mayor (Cllr A. Betton). Amongst the crowd in front of the town hall were a number of local scouts and guides. In attendance were also Mr W. G. Leggatt (District Commissioner), Fred K. Ly. R. Reygard BD (Chief Danish Scout) and Mr Lykkezard (Interpreter).

In May 1947 Admiral Sir Arthur J. Power, Second Sea Lord, inspected H.M.S. Gosling (also known as H.M.S. Scotia) at Lowton. He was impressed with the efficiency and organisation of the Signals Training Establishment. The Admiral was received by Capt. H. W. Williams, R. N. Commanding Officer. This photograph shows some of the personnel who obviously enjoyed the occasion. The site was subsequently occupied by the National Coal Board's Anderton House.

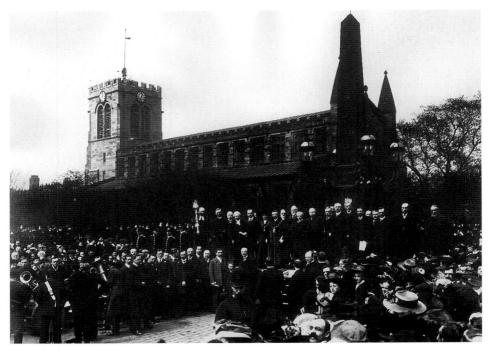

At half past twelve on 9 May 1910 crowds gathered around the obelisk in Leigh Market Place to hear the Mayor (Ald. W. J. Smith JP) proclaim George V as the new King.

Crowds gathered outside the Town Hall on Friday 8 February 1952 to hear the Mayor of Leigh (Cllr W. Woolstencroft JP) proclaims Her Royal Highness Princess Elizabeth as Queen Elizabeth II. With the Mayor is his wife and the Town Clerk, Mr A. Jones. After the ceremony a peal of bells rang out from Leigh Parish Church.

Like many other buildings in the town, the Conservative Club on Railway Road was colourfully decorated to celebrate the visit of King George V and Queen Mary. Besides photographs of the royal couple, the Club sported a banner with white letters on a purple background with the inscription 'God Bless Our King and Queen'.

On 2 June 1953, the coronation of Queen Elizabeth II took place in Westminster Abbey. Many local events were organised during this time of celebration, such as this 'queen crowning' at Hindley Green.

On 26 June 1897 a Bullock Roasting was held on Westleigh Heath to celebrate Queen Victoria's Diamond Jubilee. The bullock weighed 10cwt 3qts 14lbs and the flue oven erected by Henry Prescott measured 10ft in length, 6ft in height and 5ft 1in wide. The butcher in the bowler hat and pinafore is T. Ward.

Chat Moss Hotel, Glazebury. The decorations would suggest that celebrations were taking place in 1911 for the coronation of King George V. The building is still used as a pub today.

On 6 July 1936 the Duke of Kent visited Leigh during his two-day tour of voluntary centres for the unemployed in Lancashire. The photograph shows model yachts made by local unemployed men being examined by the Duke outside Leigh Leisure Club. The Club, which was in The Avenue, had been opened on 1 February.

King George VI and Queen Elizabeth visited Leigh on 18 May 1938. They are shown in front of Leigh Town Hall with the Mayor (Cllr P. Newton JP) and the Town Clerk (Mr T. B. Bamber).

A rare photograph of a funeral procession in Bedford Square around the turn of the century.

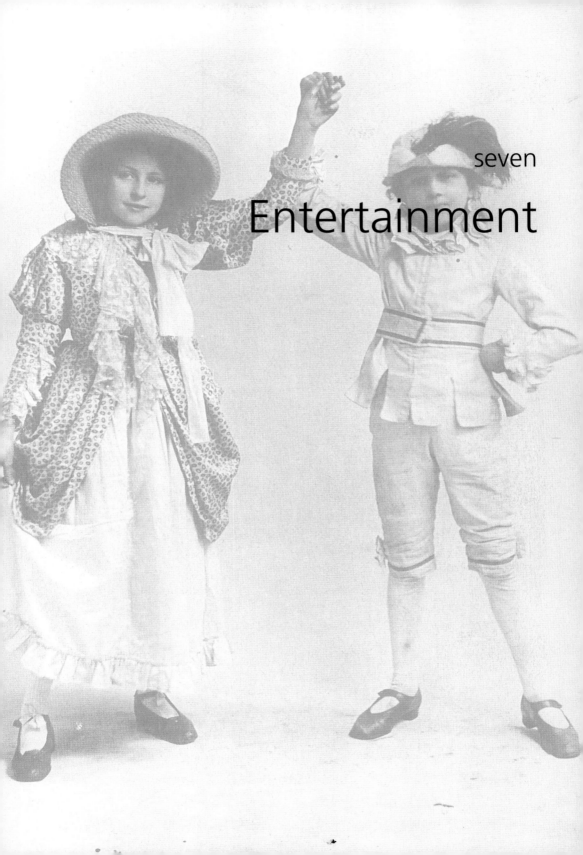

seven

Entertainment

'Revill Halls' Entertainment Troupe photographed during a show at Llandudno in the early
1900s. James Wilkinson (centre back) a local entertainer was married to Lousia (front left).
Wilkinson, a music dealer at the 'Arion' music store, Queen Street, Leigh, in the early 1900s also
gave singing lessons. In January 1910 he was Musical Director at the Hippodrome Gardens,
Llandudno, besides being Director of Leigh Male Voice Choir.

Above: Westleigh Brass Band in the mid 1880s. The band was formed in June 1881 with John Brown of Westleigh as leader. He was also bandmaster of the Blackrod Temperance Band. In 1885 the band took two first prizes at a contest at Cadishead, the test piece being the *Frost and Sun* quadrilles. Three members of the band have been identified: James Eckersley (second row, second left), Meshach Lycett (fourth from left) and Billy Manish who is holding the triangle.

Right: Two pupils at a concert given by Class VI at Leigh Church of England Girls School in December 1919.

Opposite below: On Monday 16 August 1909, Mr Charles Butt and his Royal Mandolin Band appeared at the Leigh Assembly Rooms and Picture Palace, Railway Road, Leigh. The novelty orchestra comprised twenty-four local children, directed by Mr Butt, who was also violin soloist.

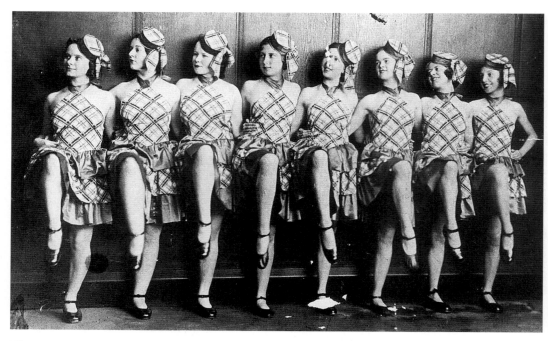

The Mauviemaids were a group of female dancers belonging to the Mauvies Concert Party. Leigh Amateur Dramatic Society (previously known as the Pennington Amateur Dramatic Society) had for many years given the Shrove Tuesday entertainment at Pennington Church. In 1922 at Bridgewater Street Schools a mixed entertainment was given by the concert party De Noir et D'Or. However the following year the name changed to The Mauvies. Mr J. L. Youd was their stage manager and producer. The photograph was taken during one of their performances in 1932.

In May 1930 the Leigh and District Girl Guides' Association held a garden party and display at 'The Firs', made available by Sir George Holden, Bart. The photograph is believed to show wand exercises by Brownies from the local Congregational Church.

A group of girls from Leigh Church of England Day School at a fancy dress dance held in the Co-op Hall. They were members of the Eurhythmic Dance team who were trying to raise money for the new school at Church Street.

Opposite below: Empire Day was inaugurated on 24 May 1902 in memory of Queen Victoria's birthday. Here a group of 'Bedford Girls' celebrate it in May 1916. This was an annual school event until the early 1950s.

On 14 March 1907 at the Assembly Rooms in Railway Road this group of children from the
Sacred Heart School performed the operetta *Zurika, The Gypsy Maid*.

Members of Bedford Church Operatic Society in February 1924 who staged one of Gilbert and
Sullivan's most popular operas *The Gondoliers*. Members of the cast included: Mr J. Grundy
(Marco), Mr Albert Schofield (Giuseppe), Miss Edna Patterson (Gianetta), Mrs Roberts (Tessa),
Miss Alice Barnes (Casilda), Mr Harold Manley (Luiz) and Mr Jack Kaye (The Grand Inquisitor).
Mr Wayne was orchestral conductor, whilst the stage managers were Mr H. Manley and Mr H.
Boardman. The scenery was painted by Mr R. Youngson.

Opposite above: St Joseph's Players added a sparkling touch to Leigh Arts Festival in June 1978
with their Summertime Revue. This colourful show at St Joseph's Hall was produced by Dorothy
Galvin. The Showtimers provided comedy and song, and The Revuettes the dance routines.

Opposite below: The Mayor (Cllr Len Sumner) with officials and prizewinners of the Leigh Drama
Festival at St Joseph's Hall, Leigh, in May 1979. The Genesians were the Arthur Crooke Trophy
winners with their play *Red Peppers* by Noël Coward. Dorothy Galvin was producer.

A scene from the stage at Leigh's first ever Bank Holiday pop festival. It was held in August 1979 at the Plank Lane Festival Site, Heath Lane. Organisers had been hoping to attract between 10,000 to 20,000 pop fans, but in the event only around 500 bothered to turn up to see 25 groups including Exodus, Supercharge and Joy Division. The first festival of its kind at Leigh had been at Bickershaw during the wet weekend of 5-7 May 1972.

eight

Sport and Leisure

First Leigh Men's Hockey Club, 1906/07 season. It was formed in November 1906 at a meeting held at the Boars Head Hotel. At this time two women's teams were already in existence.

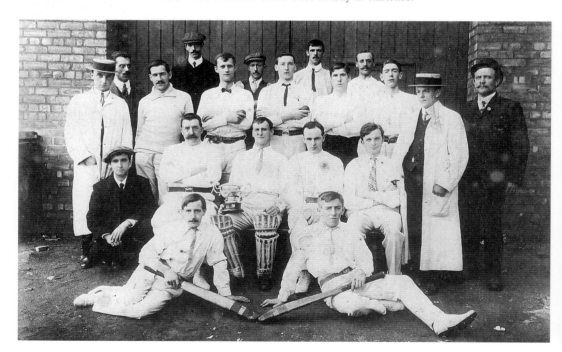

A rare picture of American servicemen from the nearby Burtonwood base playing baseball on Bickershaw cricket field, *c.*1943.

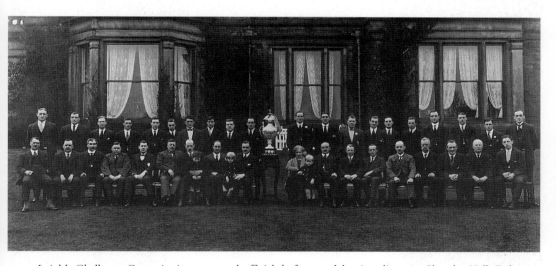

Leigh's Challenge Cup-winning team and officials before a celebration dinner at Sharples Hall, Bolton in 1921. They beat Halifax at The Cliff, Broughton 13 - 0 and became the first Lancashire side to win the Challenge Cup since 1911.

Opposite below: Anchor Cable Athletic Club Cricket Team, 1910, winners of the Leigh and District Cricket League (1st Division). Their final match to clinch the championship was against Bedford Church. Anchor scored 31 all out against a meagre 11 by Bedford Church. Members of the team in the photograph are: Back row, E. J. Gibbs (Sec.), J. R. Golden, J. Mather, T. Holmes, J. Hilton. Third row: E. Rigby, W. C. Smith, P. Wright, J. Crank, T. Tobin, H. Hampson. Second row: P. Kinsella (Cttee.), J. Bowyer, R. Higson (Capt.), F. Crooke, W. Mort, D. Jones, W. Boardman (Cttee.). Front row: L. Wood, W. Birkenhead.

The Leigh Rugby Football Club team of 1893/94 which won promotion from the Lancashire Second Competition. Left to right, back row: Ted France, J. Cheetham, J. Eccleston, J. Quirk (Hon. Sec.), Peter Taylor, John France, J. Pemberton. Middle row: F. Green, Charlie Wilding, Alf Wallwork, Tom Anderton, Tom Coop, George Boardman, Bob MacMasters. Front row: Joe Shovelton, James Shaw, Billy Ewan.

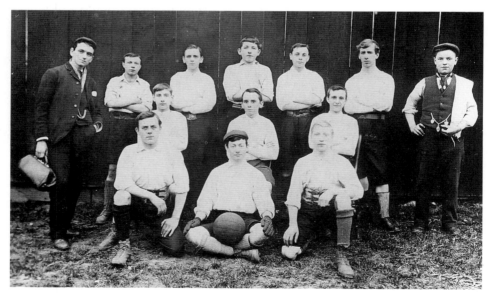

Leigh Villa Football Club, 1900/01. This photograph taken by J. Smith shows the following members, Back row, left to right: W. Slater, J. Smith, H. Johnson, T. Hilton, E. Mourice. Middle row: T. Hurst, E. Close, H. Smith, J. Watson, H. Grayham. Front row: T. Kibblewhite (Hon. Sec.), H. Ashwood (Capt.), H. Vaughan.

Leigh Boys Grammar School football team, 1928/29.

Four Lancashire champions from the Leigh Harriers and Athletic Club at their Charles Street Athletic Ground, May 1931. T. Owen from Scott Lane, Leigh, became Lancashire County Featherweight wrestling champion. Joe Reid was the English amateur wrestling bantam weight champion and English representative to the 1930 Empire games in Canada. In 1932 he also represented England at the Los Angeles Olympic Games in the bantam weight class where he finished fourth. T. Dixon was a record holding harrier and W. Jeffries a wrestler.

Left: Between the wars, Matt Thorpe of the Leigh Harriers and Athletic Club was one of the best obstacle runners in the north. Here he is seen with a selection of his trophies.

Below: Senior members of the Marsh Gymnasium Athletic team who were winners of the first Manchester and East Lancashire Amateur Gymnastic Association competition. The event was held on the 3 May 1924 at the YMCA Peter Street, Manchester. There was also a junior boy's competition as well as prizes for individual team members Altogether the teams from Marsh Gymnasium won: one competition shield, one silver cup and 14 out of 17 medals. Sir Edward Stockton presented prizes. The team members in the photograph are, standing, left to right: N. Montaro (Asst. Inst.) J. Roberts, H. Davis, W. O'Brien, A. Atherton, F. Woodward, H. Wilcock, W. Major (Inst.). Sitting, left to right: T. Scott, A. Culting, F. Williamson, F. Howard, H. Gregory.

Cllr W. Morgan (Mayor of Leigh) and his wife presenting cups to the successful competitors at the annual gymnastic display in the Marsh Gymnasium in March 1937. Miss Lavinia Charlesworth and Mr L. Gaskell were two winners. Also in the picture are Mr R. W. Richmond, Mr J. Hilton and Miss A. Smith.

In August 1938, Pennington Hall 'A' Team won the final of the Wisden Cup Tennis Championship by beating Courtaulds 'A' Team at Atherton Collieries court. The successful team are: (back row, left to right) James Hilton, D. Bratt, Jack Hilton, J. Morris, Joe Hilton, V. Murry; (front row, left to right) K. Peasnall, E. Grundy, P. Dyer, O. Needham.

Bowlers at the Hindley Green Athletic Field on Atherton Road, *c.*1920.

The BICC Anchor Cable Works sports ground which was opened in the early 1900s.

Above: A bicycle built for Mr Abbott of Leigh Cycling Club, *c*.1920. Mr Bickerstaffe (bike builder) of Warrington Road, Wigan, is sitting on the cycle. Mr Taylor, racing trainer is standing.

Right: The front page from a Leigh Grammar School Annual Sports Day Programme for 17 June 1890.

LEIGH GRAMMAR SCHOOL

ANNUAL

FIELD SPORTS,

TUESDAY, JUNE 17, 1890,

ON THE

LEIGH CRICKET GROUND,

DOWN CROFT.

President : W. E. MARSH, ESQ.

Patrons:

R. Marsh, Esq., A. McGregor, Esq., F. Le Mare, Esq., W. H. Guest, Esq., T. E. Withington, Esq., J.P.; R. T. Marsh, Esq., W. C. Jones, Esq., J.P.; J. Hayes, Esq., G. H. Evans, Esq., J.P.; W. L. Green, Esq., W. C. Freeman, Esq., H. Stout, Esq., G. Berry, Esq., B. Jones, Esq., W. B. Williams, Esq., W. Unsworth, Esq., J. Jackson, Esq., R. Bowen, Esq., E. Greenough, Esq., J. Lowe, Esq.

JUDGES:

MR. G. HORROCKS.   MR. JOHN LOWE.   MR. JOS. PENNINGTON
(White)

STEWARDS:

MR. J. BATTERSBY.   MR. W. C. FREEMAN.   MR. B. JONES
MR. R. SCHOLES.   MR. J. STOTT.   MR. WORTH. MR. YOUD.
(Blue)

STARTER: MR. J. W. BENNETT (Red)

HANDICAPPER: MR. W. H. R. DARLINGTON.

CLERK OF THE COURSE: MR. J. E. ROBERTS, (Pink)

Hon. SECRETARIES:

JOHN BERRY.   FRANK STOUT.   (Yellow.)

The PRiZES will be distributed between the Innings of the match, by REV. J. R. NAPIER. B.A.

Marks are assigned to each event as indicated herewithin.—The Athlete who obtains the highest sum of these marks will hold the Cup.

Old Boys who purpose competing in **Event No. 10**, should enter with the Clerk of the Course before 2 o'clock.

Norice.—None but officials allowed within the Ring. Boys are requested to leave the best places for visitors.

Horrocks and Sons, Princess and Bill Pystces, Leigh.

Leigh Literary Society members pictured at Ilkley on Tuesday 9 August 1892. James Ward (Secretary) in on the right. The party Leigh by train at 7.25 am and arrived back at 11.30 pm. The trip cost 13*s* 0*d* each.

On 7 May 1927, a group of amateur photographers from the Leigh Literary Society Photographic Section visited Culcheth Hall and wood. Mrs W. Prescott acted as guide.

Loafing about: four Leigh lads at Beech Walk in the early 1900s.

Messing about in boats: This trio in the early 1900s tried their hands at fishing on Pennington Flash.

A special train for the workers from BICC's Anchor Cable Works who were going on an outing to Blackpool in the mid–1930s. The train is standing in Leigh Bedford Station.

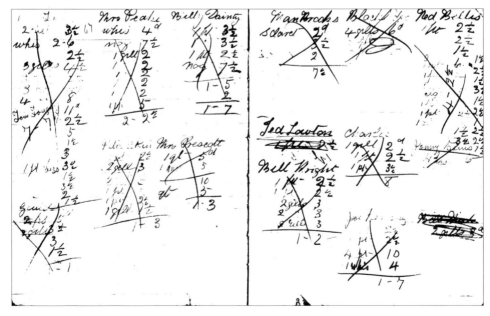

Two pages from an early twentieth century tally book for the Bowling Green Inn on Wigan Road.

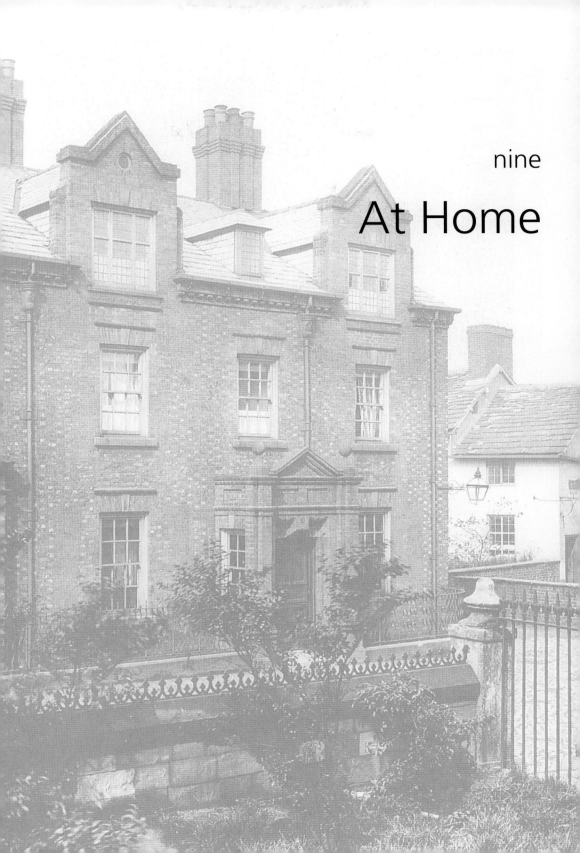

nine

At Home

The Oaklands (77 St Helens Road, Leigh), photographed here at Christmas 1907, was the home of Peter Heald, whose pork butcher's business was at 31 Bradshawgate.

Terraced houses (possibly handloom weavers' cottages originally) on Atherton Road, Hindley Green, *c*.1935.

In the fifteenth century the Pemberton family held a considerable estate known as Etherston Hall. Later owners included the Leylands, Tyldesleys and Renacres. Around 1862 the estate was purchased by Thomas Jones a wealthy cotton broker who built a new Hall, the old one becoming a farmhouse. The new house (shown here) had three sitting rooms and six large bedrooms. The estate was purchased subsequently by Robert Guest (owner of Firs Lane Cotton Spinning Mill). The old hall was pulled down in 1908.

Fairfield House (now occupied by Carelink Ltd) on St Helens Road, c.1910. The householders sitting in the Edwardian motor car are probably the family of Dr William Gray, whose surgery was in Brown Street North. Previously Fairfield was occupied by Thomas Hayes, the Leigh mill owner, and in recent years has been a hotel.

The Old Vicarage, Leigh, c.1900. An elegant Georgian brick house, it was vacated in around 1948 and used subsequently as offices by the Water Department before demolition in 1972. The present vicarage was built next to it in 1959. On the right is part of Vicarage Farm, occupied then by the Cleworth family; William used the end bay as a clog shop.

Canal Farm House, opposite Stanley Cotton Mill by the Bridgewater Canal, shortly before demolition. Next to the house is Mather Lane Cotton Mills. In 1851 Thomas Abbott together with his wife Louisa and their two children lived at the farm. In 1938 Leigh Heath Committee condemned the building as unfit for human habitation.

Above: Bamber Lodge Farm, Newton Road, Lowton, in the early 1900s. The original name of the building was Green Farm. The man standing to the right of centre is Jack Ball, brother of Peter who lived in the Old Cottage, Newton Road. The remaining people are the Adamson family who farmed at Bamber Lodge.

Right: During November and December 1914 groups of Belgian refugees were received in Leigh. Many local organisations furnished houses for individual Belgian families. This one is the 'Conservative' House. Standing outside the doorway (left to right) are: Mr E. J. Smith, Mrs Carruthers, the Belgian tenants (Mr and Mrs Garcia and children, Mrs W. Morgan and Mr Morgan.

On 31 July 1909, after a deluge of rain, the river Glaze burst its banks and flooded Platt Street East, Mr Prescott's builders yard and the Leigh Church Football Field. Here a local resident is conveyed to safety possibly by Mr Boydell of the Brown Street Ironworks.

Kitchen in a house at Shuttle Hillock, Westleigh before clearance orders were made for its demolition in 1932.

A rare photograph of the inside of a pre-war Leigh council house, mid-1930s.

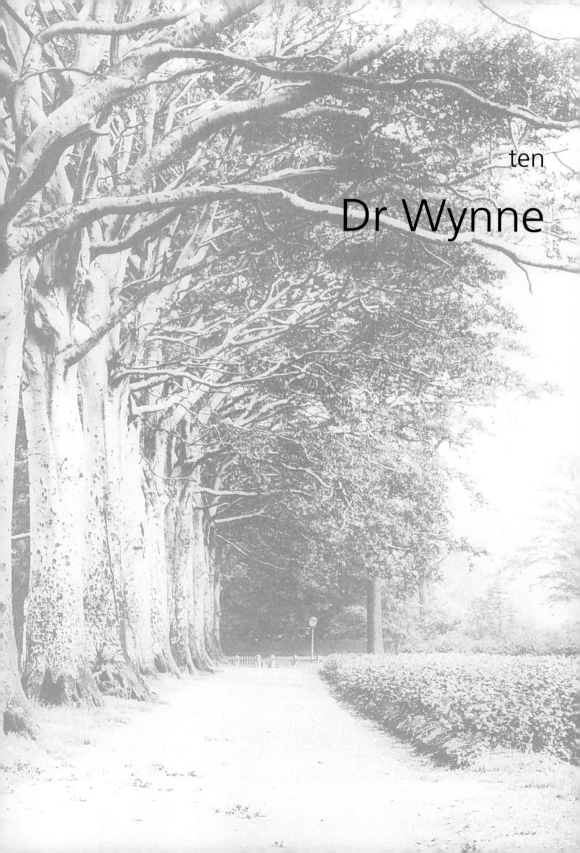

ten

Dr Wynne

Left: Frederick Edward Wynne (1870-1930) was born in Ireland, son of the Bishop of Killaloe. Educated in medicine at Dublin and Manchester, he held hospital appointments and was in general practice before moving to Leigh in 1896. He was appointed as the Borough of Leigh's first full time Medical Officer of Health. In 1911 he took up a similar appointment at Wigan before moving to Sheffield in 1921 where he finished his career. Between 1904-07 he was an active member of the Leigh Literary Society, helping to found its dramatic section. He also edited the short-lived *Leigh Courier*. He was also a playwright and photographer and this section is a celebration of prints taken from his lantern slides of the Leigh area dating from *c*.1905.

Below: Leigh Parish Church and the backs of Vicarage Square, from Bengal Street. The gate admitted the footpath to Vicarage Square. The stone flag fence enclosed the Bowling Green and the second building from the right is the Walmesley Arms, listed in contemporary directories as being located at 22 Market Place. Bengal Street was paved in 1906.

Above: A fine view of Back Salford Street probably taken from the Assembly Rooms or Conservative Club. The Parish Church can be seen in the background and the King's Head at top right. The building with gable-end window was an eighteenth century Sunday School. Just out of the picture to the right is the rear of the Congregational Sunday and Day School whose entrance was in Newton Street. The houses were demolished before the end of the war and the site is now the car park at the side of the Town Hall.

Right: Another view of the tower of Leigh Parish Church from Vicarage Square. The building to the left is the old Walmesley Arms. Edmond Seddon senior was the publican at this period.

A view of Pennington Flash looking towards Bickershaw Colliery. The emergence of The Flash due to mining subsidence around around 1900, on a river recognised as 'liable to floods' was still a very recent memory for Leythers.

Rural tranquillity. A scene at Glazebury showing the River Glaze.

Great Fold, Marsland Green, Bedford, by the Bridgewater Canal. It is mentioned in a probate inventory dated 1639. By the late eighteenth century there was a main house with several cottages adjoining. By 1891 it was divided into ten numbered properties. Several of the householders were living on private means, the others being a farmer, a clerk, and a book-keeper.

Another view of one of the Great Fold properties. The lane in front of the house joined Manchester Road. Opposite the junction was the lodge and driveway to Leigh Cemetery which was consecrated in September 1856.

Lions Bridge in ruins. On 15 April 1863 James Smetham (an artist who was friendly with Dante Gabriel Rossetti) was visiting his mother at Platfold and in one of his letters to William Davies wrote, "I am just by Atherton Bridge, with its broken lions and sphinxes and the pool choked with water lilies, reeds and rushes. It seems as if one could never ponder long enough among these old scenes – old even to me".

Yew Tree Farm (formerly Urmston's) at Landside, Pennington. This is a rare view of a traditional farm yard showing a wagon next to the tall hay rick on the right. The timber-framed barn at left is of some antiquity. James Lythgoe and his family occupied the farm at this period.

Opposite below: Yew Tree Farm, Landside; note the mounting block by the gate and the unusual heart-shaped gable decorations. Dr Wynne wrote of Landside, "The time to see Landside is one of those clear, windy November afternoons, following rain when the floods are out in the fields and the autumn glow is concentrated in the west to deepen the sunset fires. Then the spirit of the place seems to brood gently over it, pregnant with memories of an eventful past and common objects shine with unsuspected colours".

A picturesque roofscape in Westleigh. These old buildings overlooked the vacant ground between St John's Mission Church and Leigh Road by the Co-operative shop at the corner of Kirkhall Lane.

An unidentified location showing Dr Wynne's interest in the artistic arrangement of old roofs and chimneys. The chimney on the left probably belonged to one of the many mills that have now been demolished.

Reminiscent of Wordsworth's *Solitary Reaper* this photo captures an idyllic though unidentified rural scene near Leigh.

Hall House, Bedford, near the Bridgewater Canal. At this period the Hall was occupied by William Harrison, engineer, and the farm (shown here) by Samuel Eckersley. Early in the nineteenth century there had been a cotton mill and log factory here, together with Hall Houses mill, which in 1856 had a water wheel and steam engine for motive power.

Beech Walk, Pennington was a country lane planted with beech trees in the nineteenth century. Even in Edwardian days pollution could be seen by the pock marks on the bark, together with the initials of numerous Leythers.

Personalities

Above left: Hezekiah Close was renowned throughout the theatrical world as a drummer and tympanist. He was a native of Leigh and began work at Butts Foundry before becoming a fitter at Harrison McGregor's Albion Foundry. Whilst there he became a drummer at Leigh Theatre Royal and then joined a touring variety company. He was professionally known was 'Ki' and toured Spain with Cochran's Revue and Canada with St Hilda's Band. In 1928 he became licensee of the Spring View Inn. 'Ki' died in June 1950. The night before his death he had performed with the Warrington Royal Court Theatre Company.

Above right: J. B. Gough, the celebrated advocate of Temperance delivered an oration on 5 July 1855 at Leigh Wesleyan Chapel. A large audience paying between 1s 0d and 1s 6d heard him argue forcibly against the fatal consequences of drunkenness and imploring all concerned to prevent the spread of this scourge. The meeting was a great success. After the cost of expenses had been deducted a balance of £7 5s 0d was handed to the treasurer of the Leigh Temperance Society.

Opposite above: In 1931 the Cotton Queen of Great Britain was Miss Lois Heath from Tyldesley who was employed as a card tenter at Atherton's Laburnum Mills. In August she attended a garden party in the grounds of Leigh Infirmary and this is probably where the photograph was taken, with a large marquee as the backdrop. In 1940 Lois married George Hartley; she died aged seventy-nine in 1994 and was buried at Atherton Cemetery.

Opposite below: Hezekiah Close's motor engineering shop on Railway Road around 1924.

Charles Clement Abbott who lived at Astley and practised as a herbalist at his Railway Road dispensary in Leigh died in November 1983, aged ninety-four. For over sixty years he had clashed with coroners and was frequently in dispute with medical opinion over his beliefs and herbal treatment. Abbott was a vegetarian all his life and his interest in herbal remedies began when he was seventeen. In the notorious 'Black Box' case of 1931 Abbott was acquitted of the manslaughter of an eleven-year-old boy who died of meningitis. The judge said that Abbott "treated the boy according to his theories and there was evidence to show that he improved. There was nothing to show that the prisoner accelerated the boy's death in any way". The herbalist business is still being carried on today at 56 Railway Road.

Wilfred Pickles once intimated that there was "no reason at all for the widespread notion that Bournemouth is superior to Bolton, or Leamington better than Leigh". In March 1951, together with his wife Mabel this well loved radio personality undertook a three-day tour amongst the miners of Leigh and District. Whilst at Leigh he attended the Co-operative Hall to do a 'Have a Go' programme in front of a large audience. During his tour he met local coal rippers Billy Lyon and Tommy Calland from Chanters who were photographed with Ethel Gill, a screen hand from Atherton.

A picture from the Miners' Gala, June 1967. George Woodcock (General Secretary of the TUC) is at the microphone. Also on the platform are Bessie Braddock MP, Harold Boardman (Leigh's MP), Cllr L. K. Crossley (Miners' Union President), Cllr J. Shuttleworth (Mayor) and Sid Vincent (Miners' Agent). The event was held on the Marsh Playing Fields.

Peter Kane who lived at Golborne was born in Heywood (between Rochdale and Bury) in 1918. He served an apprenticeship at the Kenyon Lane Smithy, Lane Head, Lowton. Here he is seen in the 1930s striking for Chris Jordan the blacksmith. His blacksmithing work helped to develop the muscle power which made Peter such a big hitter. His boxing skills became polished through appearing in the boxing booths. At the age of sixteen he turned professional. He lost none of his first forty-one fights. In September 1938 he beat Jackie Jurich at Liverpool to take the World Flyweight Championship. When war came he joined the RAF. It was almost five years before he could defend his crown, without success. He retired at the age of thirty in 1948 and died in 1991.

Thomas Aspinall Burke was born at 7 Mather Lane, Leigh, on 2 March 1890, the son of an immigrant Irish miner, but descended on his mother's side from an old Leigh family - the Urmstons. Tom began his singing career in the children's operettas put on by St Joseph's R.C. Church, and he later joined the choir. His debut in opera was made at the Lyric Theatre, Milan, singing lead tenor in *Rigoletto*, followed by performances in Palermo, and in a new opera by Mascagni, *La Lodaletta*, in Rome, where he impressed Dame Nellie Melba, who was sitting in the audience. His first operatic appearance in England was at the re-opening of the Royal Opera, Covent Garden, where he sang Rodolfo to Melba's Mimi in *La Boheme*. He is pictured with his first wife Marie on the *Carmania* in 1920 en route to America. Returning to England he made concert appearances, forming his own concert party in 1933, and also made four films. He came back to live in Leigh after the Second World War, but went south later in life, when he took up teaching. His first wife Marie Burke was also a good singer, as was their daughter Patricia. He died on 13 September 1969.

Clive Powell was born on 26 June 1943 in Leigh. His home was in Cotton Street. This musical entertainer's stage name, however, was Georgie Fame and was known as 'The boy with the Ray Charles sound'. In December 1964 he had his first No.1 hit with *Yeh Yeh* which was in the charts for 12 weeks. Amongst his other hits were *Get Away* another No.1 in June 1966 and the *Ballad of Bonnie and Clyde* in December 1967 which also reached top position. His backing group was called the All Flames and he toured with the Irish musician Van Morrison.

Ken Platt was born in the Plank Lane area of Leigh. In his early variety years, when this photograph was taken, he played the ukulele and was constantly compared to George Formby. As he did not like to be seen 'aping' Formby he decided to become a comedian, whilst still retaining his job in the stranding department of Callender's Cable Works. He starred in *Stars in Battledress* in Italy and after demobilisation returned to help run his parents' grocers shop. He met Ronnie Taylor, a BBC scriptwriter who was also from Leigh, who arranged for him to have a BBC audition. He starred in such shows as *Over the Garden Wall* with Norman Evans, *Variety Playhouse* and *Educating Archie*. His well known catchphrase was 'I won't take my coat off, I'm not stopping'.

This 1907 postcard, depicting an 'express', was drawn by Cynicus. It appears to have been a general postcard, on which has been stencilled 'From Leigh'. Cynicus was the pseudonym of the Scottish satirical artist Martin Anderson (1854–1932).

Acknowledgements

The author is grateful to the following for allowing photographs in this book to be reproduced:

Bert Worsley, the Wynne family, the Close family, Mrs Manfredi, Mrs Cyril Ward, J. Twentyman, Tom Carroll and others.

Thanks also to Alastair Gillies, Heritage Services Manager for suggesting this project, and Len Hudson of the Heritage Service for the photography and to Stephanie Tsang.